# DEMYSTIFYING DISCUSSION

JENNIFER ORR

# DEMYSTIFYING DISCUSSION

How to Teach and Assess
Academic Conversation Skills, K-5

Arlington, Virginia USA

2800 Shirlington Road, Suite 1001 • Arlington, VA 22206 USA
Phone: 800-933-2723 or 703-578-9600 • Fax: 703-575-5400
Website: www.ascd.org • Email: member@ascd.org
Author guidelines: www.ascd.org/write

Ranjit Sidhu, *CEO & Executive Director;* Penny Reinart, *Chief Impact Officer;* Genny Ostertag, *Managing Director, Acquisitions & Editing;* Julie Houtz, *Director, Book Editing;* Mary Beth Nielsen, *Editor;* Thomas Lytle, *Creative Director;* Donald Ely, *Art Director;* Samantha Wood, *Graphic Designer;* Keith Demmons, *Senior Production Designer;* Kelly Marshall, *Production Manager;* Shajuan Martin, *E-Publishing Specialist*

Copyright © 2022 ASCD. All rights reserved. It is illegal to reproduce copies of this work in print or electronic format (including reproductions displayed on a secure intranet or stored in a retrieval system or other electronic storage device from which copies can be made or displayed) without the prior written permission of the publisher. By purchasing only authorized electronic or print editions and not participating in or encouraging piracy of copyrighted materials, you support the rights of authors and publishers. Readers who wish to reproduce or republish excerpts of this work in print or electronic format may do so for a small fee by contacting the Copyright Clearance Center (CCC), 222 Rosewood Dr., Danvers, MA 01923, USA (phone: 978-750-8400; fax: 978-646-8600; web: www.copyright.com). To inquire about site licensing options or any other reuse, contact ASCD Permissions at www.ascd.org/permissions or permissions@ascd.org. For a list of vendors authorized to license ASCD e-books to institutions, see www.ascd.org/epubs. Send translation inquiries to translations@ascd.org.

ASCD® is a registered trademark of the Association for Supervision and Curriculum Development. All other trademarks contained in this book are the property of, and reserved by, their respective owners, and are used for editorial and informational purposes only. No such use should be construed to imply sponsorship or endorsement of the book by the respective owners.

All web links in this book are correct as of the publication date below but may have become inactive or otherwise modified since that time. If you notice a deactivated or changed link, please email books@ascd.org with the words "Link Update" in the subject line. In your message, please specify the web link, the book title, and the page number on which the link appears.

PAPERBACK ISBN: 978-1-4166-3063-0 ASCD product #122003   n11/21
PDF E-BOOK ISBN: 978-1-4166-3064-7; see Books in Print for other formats.
Quantity discounts are available: email programteam@ascd.org or call 800-933-2723, ext. 5773, or 703-575-5773. For desk copies, go to www.ascd.org/deskcopy.

**Library of Congress Cataloging-in-Publication Data**
Names: Orr, Jennifer, author.
Title: Demystifying discussion : how to teach and assess academic
   conversation skills, K-5 / Jennifer Orr.
Description: Alexandria, Virginia USA : ASCD, [2022] | Includes
   bibliographical references and index.
Identifiers: LCCN 2021035882 (print) | LCCN 2021035883 (ebook) | ISBN
   9781416630630 (paperback) | ISBN 9781416630647 (pdf)
Subjects: LCSH: Thought and thinking--Study and teaching (Elementary) |
   Communication in education. | Elementary school teaching. | Effective
   teaching.
Classification: LCC LB1590.3 .O77 2021 (print) | LCC LB1590.3 (ebook) |
   DDC 371.102/2--dc23
LC record available at https://lccn.loc.gov/2021035882
LC ebook record available at https://lccn.loc.gov/2021035883

31 30 29 28 27 26 25 24 23 22         2 3 4 5 6 7 8 9 10 11 12

*This book is dedicated to all of the elementary students who have taught me how to be a better teacher and a better person. I am grateful beyond words for the time I have had with each of them.*

# DEMYSTIFYING DISCUSSION

| | |
|---|---|
| Introduction | 1 |
| 1. Shifting Mindsets | 13 |
| 2. Sharing Thinking | 40 |
| 3. Exploring Others' Thinking | 71 |
| 4. Synthesizing Thinking | 97 |
| 5. Navigating Disagreements | 126 |
| 6. The Payoff: Using Conversations for Assessment and Planning | 151 |
| Acknowledgments | 168 |
| References | 172 |
| Index | 176 |
| About the Author | 182 |

# INTRODUCTION

Learning is a social activity. Even when one is learning without anyone else around, some sort of connection with others exists—maybe through something previously built or written, heard, or seen. People inform one another's learning in many ways. We also learn directly from and alongside others. Take a moment and think about something new you learned recently. Did you learn it from reading something? From listening to the radio or watching TV or videos? Was it something you learned in a conversation with someone else?

Human beings are constructivists, constantly constructing meaning from the surrounding world. Sometimes that construction is easy and flows naturally. When we are struggling to understand something, such as another language or an unfamiliar symbol or new idea, it often helps to connect this new learning to things we already know and work to construct a meaning that makes sense and fits the context.

It is not surprising, then, that it's possible to do a lot of learning through conversations with others. This may be as simple as learning something specific that was the reason for a conversation: directions to an event, what needs to be done next on a project at work, or how someone is doing during a challenging time in their lives. Such conversations have the goal of learning certain information. At other times, conversations offer learning that was not anticipated or planned. This may come directly from the topic of the conversation or in other ways. You might learn something about the person you're talking to, something they were not even aware they were sharing through their body language, facial expressions, or word choice. You also might learn something new about a topic they are discussing. Every conversation helps you learn new things, although you may not always be conscious of them.

## What Are Academic Conversations?

Students learn a lot through conversations at school. Like adults, they learn about their peers and others in the school. They learn about interesting new subjects and ideas. Young children are constantly learning. Teachers can build on that natural curiosity and instinct to learn through academic conversations.

*Academic conversations,* as presented in this book, are student-led conversations about the academic content they are studying. These conversations may be between two students, a small group of students, or an entire class. No matter the grouping, the necessary skills and benefits of the conversation are the same.

Let's look at an example of a conversation a class of 3rd graders[*] had about *Knock, Knock: My Dad's Dream for Me* (Beaty & Collier, 2013).

---

[*] Student names are changed, but conversations are re-creations of or pieced together from a variety of transcripts and conversation maps.

**Kenia:** The dad is never going to come back because he wants the boy to learn and the boy misses his dad.

**Aikumush:** You have to let go as you grow up.

**Kimberly:** Dad was teaching the kid to do some things.

**Jefferson:** Yeah, the dad wanted the boy to grow.

**Marvin:** That's why his dad sent him the letter. Because he won't be there, and he has to learn on his own.

**Kenia:** I agree with Jefferson. He didn't want the boy to be like a baby.

**Jefferson:** His dad was guiding him, and he should guide himself because his whole life he won't be with him.

**Denis:** His dad's dream was that he can do his own stuff.

**Lina:** This book teaches that you need to learn to do things by yourself.

**Isaias:** That's why his dream was for his son to learn some things on his own.

**Rameen:** Right, the dad wants his son to act older and be smarter.

**Daniela:** I agree with Rameen. Maybe his dad wants him to learn by himself and just go and go. Maybe this happened to the author or illustrator.

**Lina:** Maybe the dad left because he already taught his son enough.

**Denis:** But it was hard for the dad to not tell his son he was leaving. That doesn't make sense.

**Kenia:** So the dad didn't want to leave.

**Alejandro:** His dad was guiding him because he wouldn't be with him. But he wanted to be with him.

**Nicky:** No matter what, if a person from your family left, you'll still remember them on the inside.

In student-led conversations, the teacher is not directly involved or is involved as little as possible. The conversations are not driven by teacher prompting throughout. The teacher can get the academic conversation started with a provoking question or a problem, but then steps back and allows students to talk directly with one another, rather than through interactions with the teacher. In this conversation, I read the book aloud to the class, stopping at different points to allow students to share their thinking. At the end of the book, I asked, "What do you think is the big idea of this book?" You can see that I did not speak again during the conversation.

Eventually, students may have academic conversations that never involve a teacher in any way. As students master the skills necessary, they can—and, it is hoped, will—engage in academic conversations with classmates and others when something strikes their interest. This interaction does not eliminate the need for teacher-initiated conversations to push students to discuss other topics, and it helps students move forward on the path of independent learning for life.

Children engage in conversations all the time. They discuss movies they saw recently, friends they know, something that annoyed them, and their plans for the future. Academic conversations share many similarities with the conversations children engage in on a daily basis. One of the challenges in academic conversations, however, especially for young children, is that they often are quite competent at talking with others but are not aware of the "talk moves" and skills they are using to do so. Their conversation skills have developed gradually over the years and are not something they think about. As a result, when they are engaging in discussion about a challenging topic (as opposed to the video game they played last night or what they want to do at recess), they struggle to use the myriad skills they possess and otherwise use regularly. Their brains must work to process the ideas and content they are discussing, and that becomes the focus of the cognitive load, rather than the conversation skills. They can miss out on a lot of the learning that happens in a conversation if they are not truly hearing what their peers are sharing and taking in those thoughts to build on or to question.

Later in the year, some of the same 3rd grade students were in the classroom one morning, waiting for the school day to begin. These students ate breakfast in the classroom, so there was about half an hour as buses arrived and students ate that was fairly unstructured and open. On this morning, Chris had picked up the book *True or False: Planets* (Berger & Berger, 2010). This Scholastic series of nonfiction books is great fun. Each right-hand page features a statement, such as "Mercury is the closest planet to the sun," followed by the question "True or False?" When you turn the page, the answer is on the left-hand page, along with more information. As Chris was reading the book, Gabriel and Vy sat down on the carpet and joined him. As they read, completely independent of any adult help, they had this conversation:

**Chris:** "Mars is called the Red Planet." I think it's false.

**Vy:** True.

**Gabriel:** I disagree. That's false.

**Chris:** It's true! "Astronauts landed on Mars."

**Vy:** True, that's true. They have rovers.

**Gabriel:** No, that's false. Turn the page.

**Vy:** Oh! I was just talking about rovers.

**Gabriel:** Yeah. There were rovers but no astronauts, so it's false.

**Chris:** "Jupiter is the largest planet in the solar system."

**Gabriel:** Yes, that's true.

**Chris:** I think. . . . [*turns page*] True, dang it.

**Gabriel:** "The greatest red spot is a giant storm on Jupiter."

**Chris:** No, that's false.

**Vy:** I find that false. What? It's true?

**Chris:** I didn't know that!

**Gabriel:** "Saturn is the only planet with rings." False. No, it's false.

**Vy:** That's false. 'Cause Jupiter has it too.

**Chris:** Yeah. That's right. Not just Saturn.

These students added to their knowledge about the solar system from the book and from one another. They listened to one another, agreed and disagreed, and added to the others' thinking as well as to what they were reading. Those conversation and thinking skills will serve them well in many different settings and for a long time.

# Why Should Students Engage in Academic Conversations?

The benefits of academic conversations are varied and wide-ranging, for both students and teachers. They help students grow several different skills, including social-emotional learning, listening, and thinking skills. Academic conversations also develop students' college and career readiness and their preparation for participation in their civic responsibilities (Hattie, 2012; Jerald, 2009). This book will address all of these benefits in different ways.

It is worth mentioning, in addition, that engaging students in academic conversations also supports many state standards. The National Council of Teachers of English and the International Reading Association have published and updated standards for literacy since 1996. Two of these are clearly addressed when students engage in academic conversations. One reads, "Students adjust their use of spoken, written, and visual language (e.g., conventions, style, vocabulary) to communicate effectively with a variety of audiences and with different purposes." Another states, "Students use spoken, written, and visual language to accomplish their own purposes (e.g., for learning, enjoyment, persuasion, and the exchange of information)." The strategies throughout this book are designed to help students communicate effectively and for the purposes of learning and exchanging information.

The standards I know best are those from where I teach, in Virginia (Board of Education, Commonwealth of Virginia, 2002). Starting in kindergarten, Communication and Multimodal Literacies standards guide these students as they build their oral communication skills. They must "initiate conversations"; practice "taking turns and staying on topic"; and "ask how and why questions to seek help, get information, or clarify information." All of these standards are addressed in this book: initiating conversations in Chapter 2, staying on topic in Chapter 4, and asking questions in Chapter 3. Such standards fit naturally in the work you and your students will be doing surrounding classroom conversations.

Grade-level standards continue to grow and develop; by 3rd grade, students will "use active listening strategies" (see Chapter 3), "orally summarize information" (see Chapter 4), and "participate in collaborative discussions," which is a great way to explain the big idea of all of this work! The standards for 5th graders add ideas about verbal and nonverbal clues (you'll find those in Chapters 3 and 6) and about "connecting comments to the remarks of others," a big idea you'll explore in Chapter 4. No matter where you teach or the age of your students, developing their oral language skills will be somewhere in your standards and expectations. By engaging your students in authentic and meaningful academic conversations, you will be meeting those standards.

## Why Is This Book Needed?

Students can learn to use their conversation skills in meaningful ways by first becoming aware of the skills they already have and then learning to use those skills in academic conversations. Finally, you can teach them the strategies they need to be better able to use conversations as a tool for learning and growth.

Students' ability to use their conversation skills in ways that support their learning benefits them in a variety of areas. For one thing, it will help them immediately. Talking with peers about their learning (or talking with their families or others) forces them to process their learning and build on it. Students cannot discuss their thinking about the content and skills they are learning without deepening their understanding and growing new synapses in their brains. Academic conversations result in stronger, more meaningful, and lasting learning for students (Alexander, 2018). Reflect on your own conversations: how does talking about something challenging help you to better understand it?

Second, increasing students' skills in academic conversations will help them in the long term. Being able to engage in thoughtful, thought-provoking conversations with others is a skill that students will need in college, in careers, and in their daily lives. Learning these skills early and continuing to use and refine them over time will lead to greater college and career success. The earlier students begin to develop and master these skills, the more likely they will be able to use them well as they get beyond K–12 schooling.

Finally, students who are able to converse with others in ways that help everyone learn and grow will become highly functioning citizens. Fully participating in society, working, raising a family, voting, and so on require some basic knowledge as well as the ability to continue to learn throughout life. The ability to engage in productive, open conversations about any topic and learn from others in the discussion is a benefit to all.

All of that said, academic conversations can be challenging, especially for younger students. Their lack of true understanding of the conversation skills they are regularly using makes these discussions more difficult. Young students are not fluent with complex conversation skills and need opportunities to practice them. Building fluency with these skills will allow students to use them in conversations about increasingly complex content.

Some students may also feel uncomfortable or fearful about speaking up during conversations in the classroom. This fear may stem from lack of confidence about the content being discussed, a general lack of belief in themselves, or simply the extremely common fear about public speaking. Regardless of the cause of this discomfort, it can be quite real for many young children, just as it is for many who are not so young. Developing an atmosphere of trust and risk taking in your classroom will make it possible for all students to actively participate in these conversations.

Students might also lack the strong social-emotional skills that they need for challenging conversations. The five competencies identified by the Collaborative for Academic, Social, and Emotional Learning (CASEL, 2021b) are self-awareness, self-management, social awareness, relationship skills, and responsible decision making. All of these competencies play a role in academic conversations. Students who find any of these competencies a challenge are more likely to encounter difficulties in participating in academic conversations. Supporting students' social-emotional development is part of supporting their progress in conversation skills, and both types of supports will be linked together throughout this book.

Another challenge for young children is the intense cognitive load they carry when participating in meaningful conversations about complex content and ideas. It is extremely hard for students to manage when both conversation skills and content are challenging. Think of young children learning to write; they may struggle to organize their ideas and present them in meaningful ways because they are also working to be sure their letters are formed well and their words spelled correctly. The cognitive load can simply be too much to bear. Teachers must help students focus on one piece—either conversation skills or content—until it is fluent and comfortable. Then they can raise the cognitive load in that area.

Obviously, students in the earliest years of school will face different challenges in engaging in academic conversation than will their older counterparts. If you have ever spent time in a kindergarten classroom or around 5-year-olds, you know that their conversations on any topic can be limited in sophistication. They are still developing language and the skills to use it. They need different strategies and support than do students in the upper elementary grades or older because older students have used conversation skills on a regular basis for a longer period of time. Similarly, students who have had specific support in conversation skills, either in school or elsewhere, need support in different ways than students for whom this work is new. Students in 3rd or 5th grade who have never had structured instruction or modeling of conversation skills need a different path than peers who have been practicing since kindergarten.

Throughout this book you will encounter conversations from kindergarten, 3rd, and 5th grade classrooms. Although students may need different levels of support at different ages or with different amounts of experience, the skills and strategies and approach are much the same. The end goal also remains the same no matter the age: students who are able to independently use their conversation skills to continue learning and growing.

## How Is This Book Organized?

All students, no matter how young or what their native language may be or whether or not they have a learning disability, can participate in academic conversations and use those conversations to grow their own learning and understanding of content, skills, and the world around them. By the end of this book, teachers will be able to use student-led academic conversations in their K–5 classrooms on a regular basis. Teachers will have strategies for modeling a variety of conversation skills and teaching lessons specific to different skills. In addition, they will know ways to help students refine the conversation skills they have already and those they are learning to use. Teachers will have a toolkit for assessing these skills as well as using academic conversations as an assessment tool for content learning.

To begin, this book addresses how to shift mindsets, for both teachers and students, to build a culture of trust and risk taking in which students are able and willing to participate in student-led academic conversations and learn from them. Chapter 1 focuses on developing such a culture and on the importance of students' social-emotional learning as a part of that. Chapters 2–4 lay out the specific conversation skills students need to learn: sharing one's thinking with others, exploring others' thinking, and synthesizing the thinking being shared. In addition to identifying and exploring these skills, these chapters include strategies you can use in your classroom to teach the skills and help students develop them more deeply. Chapter 5 explores how students can use their social-emotional skills and all of the conversation skills discussed in the preceding chapters to navigate disagreements. Not all conversations will be easy for the participants. Students need skills to assess their own thoughts and ideas when these differ from their peers. Chapter 6 digs into the payoff for all of this work by helping you assess how well students learn content through their classroom conversations.

Developing conversation skills in ways that will serve students for many years is not something that happens in a day. It requires time and practice, but the result will be students with stronger social-emotional skills and tools for learning independently throughout their time in school and beyond.

# 1

# SHIFTING MINDSETS

Academic conversations can only truly happen in a meaningful way in a place of trust and risk taking. This may sound obvious and relatively simple. It is not. In an elementary classroom in a typical school year, students and teacher have 180 days together. Those days are broken up by weekends and holiday breaks. Building an atmosphere of trust among the 20–30 people in a classroom is a crucial and challenging task, especially with all of the other demands on teachers at school. It is also a task that needs to be started immediately and achieved as quickly as possible, and one that requires maintenance throughout the year. Having the right mindsets—both teachers and students—is essential to building this environment.

Some of these mindsets are specific to teachers. **Trusting in students** and **letting go of control** are both important and (at least sometimes) difficult. Some mindsets, meanwhile, require development for both teachers and students. Everyone involved needs to be able to **see the benefits of mistakes** and **value questions,** especially when no one knows the answers. Finally, **strengthening social-emotional learning skills** is essential to setting everyone up for success.

The traditional model of school is one of the most significant challenges to building an environment in which students feel comfortable taking risks, admitting what they don't know, and asking questions. The majority of talk that happens in classrooms today follows the IRE model: initiation, response, evaluation (Mehan, 1979). The teacher initiates an interaction, typically by asking a question, then chooses a student to respond to the question or prompt. After the child has responded, the teacher evaluates the response.

This model continues again and again, student after student, day after day, in many classrooms. Such interactions leave no room for mistakes or lack of knowledge. When students know that their responses will be evaluated immediately, and judged as right or wrong, they internalize the importance of being "right." How often do you use this model in your classroom? There may be times when this is exactly what you desire, but if IRE is the model students know best and see most frequently, it will discourage them from gaining the confidence, skills, and comfort they need to engage in meaningful academic conversations. Instead, students will spend their time and energy working to ensure they have the correct answer at all times or trying hard never to be called on in the classroom. For many of us in education, this is what we knew as students, so it is what we continue as teachers. It doesn't have to be that way.

## Trusting in Students

As a teacher of young children, I often find myself thinking, "They can't do that" or "They aren't ready for that idea yet." This happens in spite of the fact that my students have shown me, time and time again, that I underestimate them. I have found this to be true as a teacher and as a parent: I make assumptions about children's abilities or readiness and then find them going far beyond my expectations.

As a teacher, you have certainly heard the message that you need to set high expectations for children. Setting high expectations does a couple of things. It communicates to students that you believe in them, that you think they are capable and smart (Weinstein et al., 1982). These are powerful ideas to convey to young children. It also keeps you from wasting time. If students are not quite ready or able to meet those expectations, you can always step back and give them more support by differentiating. Maybe they need a little more time to practice a skill or more one-on-one time with you to get to where they need to be. But if they are ready? Then you're moving fast. You don't need to take time to go over paths your students have already traveled; you're moving them on to new and more challenging things.

As your students begin to engage in academic conversations, you must trust in them. Believe in their abilities to develop this particular skill and to grow as independent learners. Let them try out new ideas and give them time and space to fail and to try again. If you step in every time they are struggling, they will not learn to overcome when things are difficult. Watch the struggle, listen to their ideas, and be ready to plan lessons that will help them work through misunderstandings or difficulties.

Using your classroom conversations as a tool for ongoing assessment and to drive instruction will be addressed in more detail in Chapter 6. Immediately taking over or telling them answers will only support your young learners in the short term. Trust them (and yourself) to make the journey to deeper learning.

## Letting Go of Control

The idea of letting go of control flies in the face of all of the university classes and professional development workshops on classroom management. I'm not suggesting chaos or anarchy. I do believe in the classroom as a benign dictatorship. You, as the teacher and adult in the room, are ultimately in charge. At any time, you have the capability and the right to step in and control things. However, stepping back and not controlling *everything* can shift the atmosphere in your classroom. This is part of trusting in students. When you believe in your students to do well and do right, you do not need to control everything.

One way to let go of control is to talk less. I consciously remind myself of Aaron Burr's line in *Hamilton* (Miranda et al., 2016), "Talk less, smile more." (His reasoning may be quite different, but the big idea is valid.) The more you talk, the less space your students have in which to talk. There is more, though. Adults—and especially teachers—are powerful authority figures for young children. When you speak, there is weight behind everything you say, simply because you are an adult and a teacher. If you want students to value their own voices and their own knowledge, step back and give them the space to practice. Give them your silence and let them try being the expert by sharing their ideas and knowledge.

During classroom conversations, my goal is to not speak beyond setting the prompt or question at the beginning and bringing things to a close at the end. I rarely make that goal, of course, but having that goal definitely limits how often I speak up. Throughout this book, I will share situations and times when it's important to interject in academic conversations—and why. Just bear in mind that you must have a very good reason to speak because otherwise you might not reach your goal of releasing control of the conversation and moving to student independence.

Another way to let go of control is to start the year with blank walls. If that feels too unwelcoming to you, post signs around your room that say, "Ready for Construction." Blank walls at the beginning of a school year allow you and your students to construct your learning space together. You and your students will create charts together to document their learning and to remind yourselves of ideas and strategies. As you develop them together, those charts can take the place of your "Ready for Construction" signs.

One note about the physical space of your classroom: If possible, have an open place on the carpet for your class to gather together. A space where all of your students can sit in a circle (or rectangle or oval) and be able to see one another will make conversations easier and more comfortable. One year my students watched a short video and then discussed it. They were all sitting on the carpet, facing the board, to see the video. When it was over and they began talking, the conversation stagnated quickly. After waiting a bit to see if they would get it moving, I asked them what they needed to be able to talk. Did they need to see the video again? Did they need some time to write about their thinking? One student looked up and said, "I think we need to move so we can see each other." They all quickly moved, and the conversation flowed.

## Seeing the Benefits of Mistakes

Helping students change their thinking about mistakes requires some serious work. Even by 2nd or 3rd grade, many children have learned that mistakes are shameful and should be avoided at all costs. One thing that teachers can do to shift that thinking is to **model** making mistakes. This is easy because everyone makes mistakes. You simply need to allow students to see you do so, highlight these mistakes, and model for students how to respond when one has erred.

Modeling is a strategy that I return to often throughout this book. Teacher (and student) modeling offers students examples with language that promotes trying new things or—especially in this case—shifting their thinking. The second thing you can do is to celebrate students' mistakes. The ways you respond when others make mistakes teaches students quite a bit. Positive **noticing and naming**—noticing when students make a mistake and naming it—encourages ongoing learning. This is work that must begin early and continue all year. As Mary Anne Buckley noted in *Sharing the Blue Crayon: How to Integrate Social, Emotional, and Literacy Learning* (2015),

> People judge and form attitudes quickly; it is our nature. By discussing powerful emotions early in the school year, *before* those attitudes are established, we can build the foundation of our community with empathy and acceptance in place of judgment and rejection. (p. 60)

## Modeling Making Mistakes

Thursday morning started the same way every day begins in my 3rd grade classroom, with our morning meeting. That day's meeting manager led her classmates through the greeting, share, and activity (see Responsive Classroom, 2016). But, as Jalieen led the class read-aloud of the morning message, there was a snag: a typo in what I had written for them. They noticed, as they read, that it didn't make sense. I stopped Jalieen and said to the class, "That felt wrong to you, didn't it? I noticed you all paused a bit there because you realized what you were reading wasn't quite right. It isn't. I made a mistake in this message." I grabbed one of our interactive whiteboard pens and made a correction to the morning message, thinking aloud what it should have said. Then I turned the meeting back over to Jalieen, who wrapped up the reading.

This brief incident, which took less than a minute of our class time, was an important one. Certainly, my students were demonstrating their abilities as readers when they noticed the error in the text. But, more important, my young students saw that I made a mistake and that it wasn't a big deal. Not only that, but that I could admit to the mistake, work to fix it, learn from it, and move on.

They had the opportunity to see that making mistakes is a normal part of life.

When I was a new teacher, I didn't feel this way. In my first few years of teaching, I was terrified of making mistakes; I was so worried about not knowing what I was doing and not being a good teacher. When I did make mistakes (and I most definitely did), I tried to cover them up or pretend they didn't happen. I didn't want my students to realize there were things I did not know or things I was unable to do. If I made a typo in something I wrote, I pretended not to notice and hoped my students didn't either. If I called a student by the wrong name or gave them incorrect directions, I would make an excuse. If a student asked me a question and I didn't know the answer, I would make something up or quickly change the subject. I don't think I was unique or even unusual in my attitude and actions. Most teachers did not see their teachers make mistakes when they were young, so they feel uncomfortable with the idea. It took several years before I felt comfortable admitting my mistakes or lack of knowledge to my students. And it took even more years before I realized how important it was that I do so.

Now, more than two decades into classroom teaching, I admit to multiple mistakes every day. Most of them are small, like a typo. But even when they're small, I make sure that students understand that I made a mistake. Sometimes my mistakes are big, either in my eyes or in the eyes of my students. When I tell students to go to the wrong location for specials (head to the gym when actually we have computer lab), that is something my students see as a big mistake. They often quickly correct me and point out my error. I own it: I tell them they are correct and that I was wrong, and we go on our merry way to computer lab. When I make a computational error or mislabel something on a map or diagram, either my students will point it out to me, or I will catch it myself. Either way, I note the mistake, remedy it, and keep on going. I don't try to hide it or make excuses or pretend it didn't happen.

The most serious mistakes, in my mind, are those in which I am wrong about a student—times when I misjudge a student or respond to a student in a way that is less than caring, accepting, or loving. I may have told a student to stop talking when they were explaining something about the lesson to a classmate or not believed a student when they told me they were late because a teacher had needed their help. This type of mistake, ones that are about my students rather than about content, took me longer to handle well, especially publicly. In many ways, however, these are the type of mistakes it is most important to acknowledge. How you handle these mistakes teaches your students more powerfully than other mistakes because of the personal nature of the error. It can be difficult, but it is important to admit this type of mistake as publicly as you commit it, and to apologize. This not only contributes to developing students' thinking about making mistakes, but also serves a larger purpose in building the community you want. Your students must trust that you believe in them and accept them as they are if they are going to feel comfortable with risks and errors. That cannot happen if you are unwilling to admit when you make a mistake about them.

In my 4th grade classroom some years ago, I frequently chastised one of my students, Freddy. He was often talking when he shouldn't have been, walking around the room when he should have been working, or messing around with materials in the classroom that did not belong to him. None of his behaviors was dangerous or horrible, but he was consistently challenging and distracting. One day he opted to sit by his best friend, Shams, on the carpet for a lesson, a choice that concerned me, but I let them make the choice to see if they could do well together. I began an interactive read-aloud of Eve Bunting's *A Day's Work* (1997), stopping occasionally for students to share their thinking and discuss the text. As I turned to read the last few pages, I noticed Freddy whispering to Shams. I immediately put down the book and began berating Freddy for such behavior. He turned away from Shams and hung his head. Shams interrupted me, saying, "But he was just trying to explain to me what Amira had said about the grandfather. I was confused."

I had made a mistake—a big one, in my mind: I had reinforced Freddy's sense that he was always screwing up in the classroom and getting into trouble. I made it less likely that he would be willing to talk with a friend about a text in the future. Before picking the book back up, I said,

> Freddy, I apologize. I made an assumption about the talking you were doing, and I was wrong. Thank you for helping Shams understand the book and our discussion. I will try to do a better job of not leaping to conclusions and thinking before I speak in the future.

Then I picked up *A Day's Work* and finished reading it.

By making the apology as public as the rebuke had been, I made it clear to my students that making a mistake is something everyone does. Making a mistake is not shameful or life-ending. I modeled messing up, making an incorrect assumption, and hurting someone else. But I then also modeled recognizing that mistake and the pain it caused and taking steps to fix it. My students saw that interaction and saw me use a mistake as a chance to learn and grow when I shared what I would try to do differently in the future. In addition, because the mistake was about a student, correcting it and doing so publicly supported the development of my student's self-esteem rather than undermining it. I also modeled strong social-emotional skills with my recognition and apology (Sprenger, 2020). Finally, I reinforced rather than strained the trust we were continually building in one another.

## Celebrating Mistakes

Building an atmosphere in which students (and adults) feel comfortable making mistakes is a powerful step. Seeing mistakes in a more positive light is the next step. In recent years, I've discovered research in two areas that has reinforced my determination to ensure that making mistakes without shame happens in my classroom. First, it is important for teachers to understand that making mistakes actually grows one's brain. Most teachers recognize that making a mistake, noticing it, and working to correct it can be helpful to learning. Research shows, however, that making a mistake—whether it is noticed or not—increases electrical activity in the brain, firing synapses and growing the brain. Another piece, closely connected, is that when students feel comfortable making mistakes, they are likely to work harder. Jo Boaler (n.d.), citing the work of Gabriele Steuer and colleagues, noted that "when students perceived their classroom as mistakes friendly—above and beyond other aspects of their classroom environment—they increased their effort in their work" (para. 6).

A classroom that is "mistakes friendly" is a classroom that will be more conducive to student learning in a wide variety of ways. As noted above, students will be more willing to put effort into the work they are doing as learners. They will also not be as afraid of making mistakes, thereby being more willing to take risks and work through struggles rather than give up when things are challenging (Boaler & Anderson, 2018). This is an essential foundation for academic conversations. Students who see mistakes as both a regular part of learning and as something that helps them learn will be more willing to share their ideas in a conversation and more willing to listen without judgment as their peers do the same.

The mindset that mistakes are welcome and helpful can bring about a major change in thinking for both students and teachers. Mistakes can be seen as a chance to learn, a chance to grow our brains, something positive rather than shameful. Mistakes can be celebrated!

One of the strategies I often use in my classroom's math workshop is "task and share" (Lempp, 2017). In my 3rd grade classroom, at the beginning of our math workshop one November day, I gave my students a page with two problems to solve (the "task"): 372 + 215 and 528 + 370. This was at the beginning of our unit on addition and subtraction, and I did not give them any instruction on how to solve the problems. They knew they could get math manipulatives from our shelves if they wanted them.

As my students worked, either independently or while talking with friends about how to tackle the problems, I walked around the room, looking at their strategies. Keidy had gotten a set of place-value blocks and was building the numbers with these. She counted the number of blocks she had all together to find her answer. I recommended that she draw the blocks on her paper so that I would be able to see what she did when she turned it in, and I asked her if she would be willing to share her strategy with the class. At another table, I noticed Oscar solving the problems by expanding the numbers to add them. He was writing 300 + 70 + 2 and 200 + 10 + 5, then adding the hundreds, the tens, and the ones to find the total. I asked him if he would also share his strategy. Finally, Kenia was using a number line to solve the addition problems; the line started with 372, then jumped up 100, then 100 more, then 10 more, and finally 5 more, to land on 587. I asked her to share her strategy, too.

The task-and-share model allows students to see multiple strategies—and they learn about these strategies *from their peers*, who are often better at explaining to one another than teachers might be. Teachers can have too much knowledge and struggle to put things into terms and ideas that make sense for emerging learners. Keidy, Oscar, and Kenia each came up to the easel, wrote out what they had done, explained it to their classmates, and answered any questions (the "share").

However, working a problem independently can be very different from working it on chart paper in front of one's classmates. Even though Keidy had solved the problem without any errors with the blocks and drawn it on her paper, as she worked it for her peers, she accidentally drew an extra ones block. She knew as she completed the problem that the answer she was demonstrating was not the one she had gotten, but she couldn't figure out what she had done wrong. Her classmates helped Keidy identify the mistake and she fixed it. We took a moment, together, to note all the things Keidy had done correctly in the math and to brainstorm why her error may have happened. My 3rd graders could identify that the larger numbers get, the more challenging it is to keep all of the place-value blocks straight; it's easy to draw an extra one or forget one or accidentally miscount.

This type of mistake is fairly common when students are learning new strategies. Making such an error in public becomes a learning opportunity for everyone, and this is especially true when it's an error others might also make. Taking this a step further, sometimes I choose students who have an effective strategy but are not able to implement it perfectly to share as their work, too. This can be helpful for their classmates to see, just as Keidy's inadvertent error was. Only seeing perfect work from peers does not help build an atmosphere of trust and risk taking.

It's understandable to be hesitant to share students' errors in your classroom; you don't want to set any students up for failure or make them feel bad about themselves. However, when handled intentionally and in an atmosphere of trust, making mistakes can be a valuable part of students' learning process; highlighting the positives, you actually get a positive result. In this instance, although Keidy knew she had erred, she also saw how her thought process helped her classmates learn. She saw herself as an important part of our community of learners.

Seeing mistakes in this light—as something to learn from, something to see as a step forward rather than as shameful and a step backward—is helpful to all learners. Students learn not to shut down when they make mistakes, not to give up because of one error. They also learn to accept others' errors without so much judgment. When they get to that point, seeing errors as a part of learning for both themselves and others, your students are available to learn together in new ways. They will also be far more capable of sharing their own thinking in academic conversations without fear of mistakes and working to understand others' thinking to help themselves learn more. This will be especially true when students are **Navigating Disagreements** and will be addressed in more detail in Chapter 5.

## Valuing Questions

Just as you will have to work to shift your own and your students' thinking about making mistakes, you may need to do some work related to asking questions and not knowing answers. The prevalence of the IRE model quickly convinces students that their role in the classroom is to listen to the teacher's questions and answer them correctly. It does not encourage inquiry on students' part, and it definitely discourages not knowing an answer. Again, you can help students with this by modeling when you ask questions to which you genuinely do not know the answer.

This can be a challenge for many teachers, who have been conditioned and trained to ask questions to which they know the answer. But think of it in another way: students should have the opportunity to see your curiosity. You also must be thoughtful about how you respond to students when they don't know the answer to your questions and when they ask questions of their own (Fleenor, 2010). Your actions and language around questions and inquiry are powerful.

School is often about everything a student knows or is able to do. Not knowing or not having a skill is considered a deficit, a problem that needs to be solved. Imagine a young child, 2 or 3 years old; they have no shame in not knowing things. They ask question after question every day (often to their parents' chagrin). Their natural curiosity and willingness to admit what they do not know allows them to learn a lot very quickly. And then . . . they enter school and spend a lot of time being expected to *answer* questions rather than to ask them (and to answer them correctly). Not having the correct answer becomes shameful. When this is the expectation—on the part of both students and teachers—it is difficult to create an environment that is conducive to academic conversations.

Learning through conversations requires students to be willing to take risks, share their thinking, and respond to one another in ways that go beyond mere politeness. It requires a certain vulnerability. Speaking up in class, in any way, to some extent makes students vulnerable. If the answer they give is wrong, they are likely to feel foolish or embarrassed. The same can be true in academic conversations, and this vulnerability is not what students should be feeling. It isn't your goal, as an educator, to put your students in a position to feel shame for their lack of knowledge or their errors. But if you build a classroom environment that allows and encourages meaningful academic conversations, your students are unlikely to feel that sense of shame or embarrassment. If you build this kind of classroom environment, students are unlikely to see being wrong—whether themselves or others—as a cause for concern. It is just a part of learning and growing together.

Learning and growing together does require some vulnerability, but it does not require shame. Learning through academic conversations requires that students listen to one another with open minds and try to truly understand one another. One must be somewhat vulnerable to try on the ideas and thoughts of another, to see if they fit, if they make sense, if they seem right. This vulnerability doesn't have to feel uncomfortable, however. When students have a welcoming and accepting classroom culture and their own set of strong social-emotional skills, they can be vulnerable without it being a challenge or discomfort.

## Not Knowing

Like making mistakes, not knowing is something you can model for students. In the years I have spent with elementary students, I have learned a lot about the various fads that have grabbed children's attention. I can tell you a lot about Silly Bandz, Pokémon cards, slap bracelets, gel pens, Beyblades, and more video games than I can count—and, initially, I knew absolutely nothing about any of them. When my students would talk to me about these things, rather than acting knowledgeable, I would admit my ignorance and listen and learn. I asked questions about what they were telling me. I became curious about their expertise.

A former student of mine, Christian, saw me at dismissal one afternoon and ran over to tell me something. It was clear he was excited to talk to me, so I turned to give him my full attention. "I learned how to build a house, Ms. Orr!" he said. I looked at him incredulously. "You what? You learned how to build a house? How did you do that? Who taught you?" I asked. "No one taught me! I just kept trying until I figured it out!" He could see I was perplexed as I asked, "Christian, what did you use to build a house?"

Young children often begin conversations with little to no context; they assume the listener knows exactly what they know, as Christian did. Recognizing this, I now know to tell students I don't understand and ask for more information. I often do this even when

I am able to infer the context. Originally, I did so because I wanted my students to think more carefully about how they explain things or tell stories. The oral conversations they have on a regular basis are helpful practice for the craft of writing, in addition to building useful oral-language skills. I push my students to think about how to tell me stories or explain things to me more thoughtfully and with more detail. Asking students for more information also sends the message that their ideas matter and that not knowing something is common. My interest and desire to know more about what they are sharing is powerful, and they learn they have a voice in our classroom.

Christian finally realized the information he had not given me in our conversation so far. "Oh! I can build a house in Minecraft! At first I could just build it out of dirt, but now I know how to do it with wood or cobblestones." He provided more details about the steps involved in building a house in Minecraft before rushing off to get on the bus. I knew next to nothing about this topic, so I listened carefully as Christian taught me.

Young children believe the adults in their lives know everything, which can make them feel *they* should know everything. It is a gift to tell children "I don't know" when they ask about something. It is one way of modeling being vulnerable with others. Showing them that you don't know everything frees them up to feel better about what they don't know. Your students are constantly watching you and constructing their understanding about the world based on what they see. If you are unwilling to admit you do not know something, they come to believe that not knowing is a bad thing. When you admit it without embarrassment, your students learn to do the same.

When you and your students can readily admit what you don't know, you are making yourselves vulnerable and opening yourselves to learning. It is far harder to be confident in your knowledge about something and then have to change your mind than it is to not know something and learn it. Digging in your heels, drawing a line to indicate your knowledge about something (even if it's only for show), precludes a chance to learn. Accepting that you don't know something, or that you have more to learn, is a necessary vulnerability.

## Encouraging Questions

One of the science units in my 1st grade class involved exploring how different liquids do and do not mix with water. I presented the various liquids to my students: food coloring, oil, and vanilla extract. We discussed our plan to mix each of them with water, and immediately my students had many questions. I wrote all the questions on chart paper so that we could return to them after our experiments and see if we could answer them. "Will the vanilla extract still smell the same after we put it in water?" "Will the food coloring mix with water? It's called *food* coloring, not *water* coloring." "If something is clear like water, how will we know if they mixed?"

As students shared their questions and I charted them, others murmured their approval. You could hear the hum around the carpet as students listened to one another's questions and became intrigued themselves. They knew asking questions was something to celebrate, something to be proud of doing. When we returned to the questions after our experiment, we were able to answer some, but not all of them. That wasn't a problem. My students simply began discussing with friends what kind of experiments would help them find the answers to those questions.

Asking questions was something we did all the time. If we were able to figure out the answer or if someone else knew the answer, that was great. If we couldn't figure out the answer and no one else knew it, that was OK, too. It was just something for us to keep working on and thinking about. My students understood that asking questions was positive and worthwhile. The answer wasn't always the goal; sometimes simply asking the question was enough for us. It moved us forward in new ways.

Encouraging students to ask questions, whether or not they will or can learn the answers, supports students in becoming lifelong learners. Recording questions on the board or chart paper, discussing them throughout a unit, and finding answers (or not) shows students the value of their questions in their own learning. A classroom based around students' questions is a classroom of inquiry (Heard & McDonough, 2009). Students see themselves as capable of driving their own learning, initiating questions, and searching for answers. Some answers may be found through discussion with others. Asking questions and talking to others about questions are skills children can use throughout their lives. (Chapters 2 and 3 explore these concepts in more detail.)

## Strengthening Social-Emotional Learning Skills

Academic conversations require strong social-emotional skills; at the same time, academic conversations help students develop those skills. The Collaborative for Academic, Social, and Emotional Learning (CASEL) identified five competencies in this area (2021b). These competencies play important roles in academic conversations, both in supporting students' ability to participate in such conversations and in their development through such conversations. In *All Learning Is Social and Emotional: Helping Students Develop Essential Skills for the Classroom and Beyond* (2019), Dominique Smith, Douglas Fisher, and Nancy Frey wrote,

> Emotions influence learning and behavior. Much like a speed governor on a diesel engine, they regulate the speed at which information and experiences are processed. However, when emotions run too hot, the brain and body can quickly become overloaded. Children need to learn about their emotions and how to accurately name and recognize them. (p. 65)

Emotions can "run hot" for many different reasons, plenty of which students might encounter in conversations at school and elsewhere. Developing and strengthening students' social-emotional skills will enable them to be successful, even when emotions run hot.

For all of these social-emotional skills, it is important that you also take some time to notice and reflect on your own development. CASEL's "Personal SEL Reflection" (2021a), a free downloadable document, can be a helpful tool for getting started in thinking deeply about these skills. As with anything else, it is difficult to teach others something that is difficult for you. Being aware of and thoughtful about your own social-emotional learning and growth will help you support your students in these areas.

## Self-Awareness

The competency of self-awareness is complex and involves a range of skills about understanding one's own emotions and how they influence behavior. According to CASEL (2021b), these skills include "demonstrating honesty and integrity," "having a growth mindset," and "identifying one's emotions." Self-awareness, although sometimes a challenge for some young students, is important when interacting with others (e.g., in conversations). As students work on their academic conversation skills, they will develop stronger self-awareness, which in turn will help them develop stronger conversation skills. These competencies and skills work hand-in-hand.

## Self-Management

Self-management includes "abilities to manage one's emotions, thoughts, and behaviors effectively in different situations and to achieve goals and aspirations" (CASEL, 2021b, p. 2). Although the competencies are closely related, note that self-awareness involves *identifying* emotions; self-management involves *managing* them. To participate in academic conversations, students need to be aware and in some control of their emotions and responses. Participating in conversations and developing the skills needed will also help them to develop self-awareness and self-management.

Chances are that you will need some strategies for practicing self-awareness and self-management skills with your students, both for supporting classroom conversations and for the skills' broader importance. Lori Ann Copeland's *Hunter and His Amazing Remote Control* (1998) is one resource to try. In the book, Hunter realizes his brain doesn't always work the way he wants it to, and he creates his own remote control to help. He gradually adds buttons as he realizes what he needs and what might be helpful. He includes a pause button to help himself remember to stop and think before acting and a fast-forward button to help himself see the possible consequences of his actions. It's hard for Hunter to remember to use these buttons at first, but as he practices, he is able to use them more often.

As a class, you could discuss the idea of a remote control for one's brain. What would your students want it to do? You can create a large remote on chart paper or posterboard to hang on the wall as an ongoing reference. If students find the need for additional buttons throughout the year, add them! Having a large example on the wall is both a great constant reminder to students as well as a tool you can use, individually or with the whole class. You might just point to a button as a silent cue or say to students, "As we talk today, don't forget about your pause button and stop for a moment to think before you speak."

## Social Awareness

Social awareness is a similar, interpersonal skill that plays a significant role in conversations. Social awareness includes showing empathy and compassion by identifying others' feelings and perspectives and recognizing how our own words and actions can affect others. Students will be developing and practicing these skills as they listen to their classmates, as seen in Chapter 3. Social awareness also involves learning from others, which students are doing as they **Explore Others' Thinking**. It is much harder to see the internal work that students are doing when it comes to self-awareness and social awareness than it is to see more outward-facing skills like self-management. As a result, it can be more difficult to help students develop these internal skills. More ideas and support for this work can be found in the 2021 book *We Belong: 50 Strategies to Create Community and Revolutionize Classroom Management* by Laurie Barron and Patti Kinney.

## Relationship Skills

Relationship skills include the ways in which someone interacts with others, such as communicating, cooperating, and coping with social pressure and conflict. The importance of these skills in conversations is fairly obvious. Students must not only be able to communicate to participate in conversations, but also work on cooperating to give one another the opportunity to talk. Conversations offer plenty of social pressure and conflict that students must learn to navigate. Throughout this book, I highlight ways you can help students become more capable at listening and talking with others, and how this in turn supports the development of these skills.

## Responsible Decision Making

Responsible decision making includes identifying problems and weighing solutions to solve problems. This process must be done with a focus on the well-being of all. This social-emotional skill is a significant challenge for many young children. It is difficult for them not only to identify problems and assess solutions, but also to do so with the perspective of how various solutions affect others. Conversations, academic and otherwise, are wonderful opportunities to support students in developing skills that will help them as responsible decision makers.

One piece of making responsible decisions is gathering pertinent information and working to see multiple perspectives. As students practice asking questions of their classmates and inviting quiet peers into the conversation, they are strengthening their own skills for responsible decision making.

## Routine and Structure

One strategy that supports the development of students' social-emotional skills and that helps create an atmosphere of trust and respect is to hold routine "morning meetings," a component of the Responsive Classroom model (see www.responsiveclassroom .org). The morning meeting has four parts: greeting, sharing, a group activity, and the morning message (Responsive Classroom, 2016). Each of these elements plays a role in developing a collaborative, welcoming classroom space for all students as well as in developing individual students' social skills.

The **greeting** is exactly as it sounds: an opportunity for students to greet one another at the start of the day. This can be as simple as shaking hands and saying, "Good morning," or it can get far more creative (e.g., students can greet one or two others or many of their classmates). With guidance from the teacher and reminders of how to greet in kind, respectful ways, students are developing their social awareness and relationship skills.

**Sharing** is a time for students to talk about something they want to tell their peers and includes opportunities for their friends to ask them questions. This element helps students to develop self-awareness and self-management skills.

The **activity** can be one of a wide range of options, supporting academics or focused on building community, and it generally requires collaboration and teamwork. Students might play Simon Says—like games, skip counting games, or some of the games in Chapter 4 for building self-awareness. No matter what activity you choose, you will strengthen several social-emotional skills. Working together in the games requires students to be socially aware, they must use their self-management skills in turn taking, and the collaboration is strengthening relationship skills.

Finally, the teacher writes the **morning message,** which the class reads together at the end of the meeting. This also may support academics, may share information about the day or coming days, or may be focused on developing community. Again, this piece of the morning meeting supports the growth of multiple social-emotional skills. Reading the message along with their classmates helps students develop their self-awareness and self-management skills because they must be aware of their own actions and thoughts and manage their participation to be a part of the whole group, which in turn supports their social awareness.

Another important strategy for supporting the development of students' social-emotional skills is to continuously consider the various configurations for academic conversations. Students can talk with one partner only, limiting the relationship skills and social awareness they will need to engage in discussion. Conversations can also happen in small groups, which not only increases the number of people students must work with but also gives them more people to watch and learn from. Whole-class conversations are challenging in many ways, but they offer students more opportunities to sit back, watch, and listen to their peers; there is less pressure to speak up in a larger group.

## Encouraging Participation

As your students are developing these skills, they will encounter challenges along the way. One thing you will likely find is that some students will hide when their skills, in any area, are not as strong as they would like or feel they should be. This hiding will show up with both their use of conversation skills and their content-area knowledge. Students who are hiding will work to fade into the group. They will look to their peers and model their behavior on what they see others doing. That will make it difficult to assess their growth in conversation skills and academic content, but it is actually a good sign in their social-emotional growth. By observing peers and adapting to what they see, they demonstrate progress in self-awareness, self-management, and social awareness.

When you assess students' conversation skills or content knowledge, these students will likely stand out as ones for whom you struggle to collect data. Those are important data. Recognizing that students are working to hide and not be noticed is a signal to focus more specifically on them. They may need encouragement and reinforcement that they are capable of participating. They may need positive feedback frequently to help them see their strengths. They may need some small-group practice to build confidence.

Keep a few things in mind about students who are most frequently silent. Some students rarely or never speak during academic conversations. In addition, some students who are learning English may not feel comfortable or confident enough to participate actively; listening to their peers can be challenging enough. Students with anxiety, which today is at least 7 percent of students in elementary schools (CDC, 2021), also might not feel capable of speaking up. If other students invite them into the conversation, they may feel encouraged or they may feel uncomfortable.

Having established an atmosphere of trust will be foundational for this to work. If students feel encouraged by the invitation, they may share their thinking—perhaps not in that moment, but they may be more likely to speak in the future with the knowledge that their classmates want to hear from them. If the invitation makes them feel uncomfortable, it is important that they feel they can say that they do not want to share or do not have anything to share at that moment.

If students are able to respond in such a way, the conversation will continue, and the pressure will be off them.

Students who rarely or never speak during academic conversations can participate in other ways, often dependent upon the goal of the discussion. If you are collecting assessment information about content, students who do not speak can write about their thinking, before or after the conversation. Another option is to have a one-on-one conversation with your more reluctant students to offer them a chance to talk about their thinking.

Having students write about their thinking or understanding of the topic of a conversation *before* it happens can also help students for whom the goal is to increase their participation. Having something written down, already organized and put into words, can make it easier for students to speak. Such students could speak first, sharing what they wrote, or could join the conversation at another point, especially if another student is likely to invite them in. Some students will be more willing to speak just with one partner rather than in a group, so that is another option.

If the goal of the conversation is to build specific skills for communicating, it is important that all students participate. For a student who does not typically do so, this can be intimidating. Working with such students before the conversation to set specific goals (e.g., agree or disagree with two different people, ask a question during the conversation, paraphrase what someone else said) can help them have a plan for their participation.

## Civil Discourse

Throughout this book, the focus is on how to help students gain the skills to engage in academic conversations to deepen their learning about the content they are studying. Academic conversations, however, are important for reasons that are more far-reaching. The skills addressed in this book are skills students will need and be able to use throughout their lives to engage in conversations with others. The models of conversations students see quite publicly, however, don't truly fit that name. Young children might not be watching the evening news by choice, but televisions are frequently on in homes, and children have access to a wide range of information and misinformation on social media and more widely on the internet. As a result, they are aware of more than you might like to realize. They see experts and politicians and newscasters argue with one another on the news daily. They read or hear stories of neighbors arguing vehemently or about workplace dramas.

Such individuals clearly are not using the skills addressed in this book. Instead of talking to each other to learn from each other, these "conversations" seem to be people talking *at* each other and are more focused on making a point and winning over others. In this environment, it is more important than ever that teachers are ensuring students see "conversation" through another lens. Students need opportunities to talk to their peers with the goal of learning from one another. They need to be able to listen to others, to carefully consider and question what others are saying, and to try to understand. This is what it means to engage in civil discourse and should be what students are learning, even if it is not what they are seeing regularly outside school.

Nonexamples of true conversation can be powerful teaching tools. With another teacher, model such a "conversation" for students to analyze. (Or have two or three students do so if your students are capable of taking that on. They will find it great fun.) Argue without listening to each other, speak over the other person, talk at them—in short, show students exactly what society sees as conversations and ask them what they notice. Even the youngest learners will be able to identify some problems with what they see. Ask your students what the participants should have done differently. They will tell you many of the same things you want them to be doing in their academic conversations. Even if they aren't yet capable and confident in doing the things they share, they will be taking a step forward by identifying these as positive actions. Seeing nonexamples can also help young children recognize things they do not want to do. By naming conversation pitfalls, students will be more capable of avoiding them.

---

The next chapters will describe the variety of skills students need, and teachers can teach, for participating in academic conversations. These skills will help students gain independence and grow as self-supporting learners throughout their lives. To begin the work on these skills, students need a safe, welcoming environment in which they can take risks, be wrong, and ask questions without fear of shame or embarrassment. If that atmosphere does not exist in a classroom, students will not have the range of opportunities to develop their conversation skills. The work must begin with the classroom and community.

# SHARING THINKING

All conversations begin with someone presenting an idea or thought. The idea or thought might be a statement of fact, an expression of thinking, or a question. Whatever way it's presented, someone must get the conversational ball rolling. This is as true in academic conversations as it is in personal and casual ones.

Sometimes it is easy to begin a conversation; at other times, it can be uncomfortable or nerve-wracking. A number of factors affect how challenging it can be to begin a conversation—because of the people you are talking to or the topic being discussed. The importance or reason for conversations varies and can make a significant difference in how easy it can be to have a conversation.

## Who and What

Conversations with friends or family are often easily started because comfort level and history set up the conversation and support the participants. Friends or family can make it easier to engage in a discussion.

Early in the school year (or early in this work), the "who" can make it more difficult for students to begin conversations. When students don't feel comfortable with their classmates or teacher and don't have a sense of trust, conversations will be more fraught and harder to begin. Once you have shifted mindsets and established an atmosphere of trust, the people involved in the conversation should not be a factor making it more challenging to get started.

This is not always true; conversations can be difficult even with those closest to us and with whom we are most comfortable. Some topics are always challenging, no matter who is in the conversation. Some conversations also feel life-changing—conversations about important life choices (where to go to college, whether or not to take a job) or that center on relationship issues—making people hesitate to begin because the weight of the conversation is so heavy.

Topics of academic conversations tend to be fairly innocuous, especially at the elementary school level. Discussing ways in which life in ancient Mali was similar to or different from the lives students live today is unlikely to elicit strong emotions. The same can be said for reflecting on a science experiment or discussing geometric shapes. Academic content tends not to bring out the stronger feelings, and therefore the topics should be relatively easy to discuss. At times, when discussing events in history or literature, students may feel strongly, and the topic may raise the level of challenge for the conversation. This is something to keep in mind when planning for academic conversations, especially early on.

## Why

How weighty an academic conversation feels will affect how easily students get into it. This, in turn, depends on how the teacher approaches it. If the conversation is presented as a test or competition, students will be more hesitant to participate. Academic conversations must be presented and treated throughout the year as a part of the learning process. Students must recognize the value of learning from one another in these conversations. It is important that both students and teacher understand the purpose of participating in an academic conversation. Knowing the "why" can keep the conversation from feeling scary or something to be feared. In *Questioning for Classroom Discussion*, Jackie Acree Walsh and Beth Dankert Sattes explained that the goal "is not to reach a decision, agreement, or consensus on a topic, but rather to move toward collective understanding" (2015, p. 154). If students see the goal as furthering their learning, they will be more willing to engage in meaningful ways.

Academic conversations, however, can also be a powerful tool for teacher assessment. This will be addressed more later in this chapter, and it is an important reason for using academic conversations in your classroom. It is equally important, though, to understand the difference between using conversations as an assessment and using them to grade students based on participation in these conversations.

You can learn so much from listening to your students during academic conversations. Observing these conversations will help you assess students' conversation skills and identify areas of strength as well as needs to address in future lessons. Academic conversations also offer a window into students' understanding of the content. Listening to students' discussion can help you recognize misconceptions that are prevalent or to identify areas in which your class has reached mastery about a topic. (For example, one year I learned that my 3rd graders really didn't understand the relationship between rectangles and squares, in spite of what I had previously thought.) This understanding can be immensely helpful in planning future lessons or small groups—or even future academic conversations.

Teacher assessment should not be the "why" for your students or the reason for them to feel engaged in and value academic conversations. They don't even need to know the assessment is happening—but they do need to have some understanding of why they are participating in conversations in the classroom. For many students, the idea that they can teach their classmates through these conversations is a great reason. Nowhere in our traditional model of schooling—with its IRE model of interaction (Mehan, 1979)—are students given the opportunity to see themselves as experts, as teachers. This is unfortunate because students have so much to offer one another and their teachers. Students are often wonderful teachers of their peers because their understanding is so similar. Students can explain things to one another in ways that might not occur to teachers, who are far removed from their experience and their knowledge and skill level. Someone just slightly ahead, close to another in Vygotsky's zone of proximal development (1978), can make a new idea or skill more accessible.

Finally, students need to participate in academic conversations because doing so builds essential lifelong skills. Talking to others is something everyone does on a daily basis. Participating with intention and strong skills supports ongoing learning and teaching of others. Conversation skills also benefit students throughout their lives because talking with others promotes better processing of one's own thinking (Resnick et al., 2018). Talking through things can lead to better understanding. Teachers often hear students go through this process, in conferences about students' reading or writing. Even a response to a general question such as "What are you thinking about this book?" can open the door for students to talk themselves through and into deeper understanding. Your students may not be aware they are doing so, but you can help them build that metacognition through your work on academic conversations, helping them to become more purposeful in talking through their own thinking.

## Balancing the Cognitive Load

The goal of academic conversations in the classroom is to help students learn together about the content they are studying. Learning conversation skills supports this larger goal. However, learning both conversation skills and academic content at the same time is a lot to ask, especially of young children. Working on both together makes for a heavy cognitive load. As a result, it is important to consider how best to balance that cognitive load for your students to ensure they are able to work on gaining mastery of either the conversation skill or the academic content that is your current focus.

The natural instinct is to jump into teaching and practicing conversation skills immediately with whatever content is your current focus. This might look like having students participate in a discussion with their classmates about the life cycle of a butterfly. If the current unit is your students' first exposure to the life cycle of a butterfly and you are teaching students strategies for supporting their thinking through this conversation, you may want to reconsider. Choose either the content or the conversation skill as the main focus, and allow the other to be something the students already know well. If your goal is to teach students to support their thinking, have them engage in a conversation about content they have mastered.

For example, if the previous science unit was about magnets, have students practice supporting their thinking in a conversation about magnets. This allows them to focus their effort on the conversation skill, supporting their thinking, because they are comfortable and confident about the academic content. When students gain proficiency in supporting their thinking and it requires less effort for them, they will be ready to use that skill to discuss content that is more challenging.

As you plan for conversations in your classroom, whether whole class, small group, or partner talk, imagine a seesaw. One side is the academic content that will be the topic of the discussion; the other side is the conversation skill on which students will be working. Think carefully about how challenging both things are for the majority of your students. If both the content and the conversation skill are quite challenging, the seesaw will be stagnant. Both sides will be pushing down, keeping the seesaw from going up and down, and keeping students from being able to move forward in their learning. One side of the seesaw should be a challenge, however, as students will not grow if both sides are too easy.

Even when students are gaining significant proficiency with their conversation skills, there should always be some focus in that area. Do not assume that your young learners have completely mastered participating in meaningful academic conversations any more than you would assume they've completely mastered multiplication or persuasive writing. Most adults haven't mastered participating in conversations meaningfully!

If the content-area concept will be the challenging part of a class discussion, consider which conversation skills still need some refining. Remind students of this as they begin the discussion. If your students worked on supporting their thinking early in the year and are fairly good at it, they can still use some reminders to do so and to ask each other for evidence if it is not shared. These skills, just like those related to content learning, can always grow and improve.

Participating in academic conversations happens in several different ways. Students need to be able to share their own thinking and understanding with others (the focus of this chapter). They also need to be able to explore others' thinking (Chapter 3), and they must learn to use these conversations to synthesize and co-create understanding with others (Chapter 4). You can address each of these big ideas through a number of strategies to help move students to independence. For sharing their own thinking or understanding, students need to be able to **initiate** conversations, **support** their thinking in conversations, and **clarify** what they are saying and thinking.

## Initiating Conversations

To get started with academic conversations, you, as the teacher, will set up the conversation. You might begin by asking a question of your class or offering a scenario to discuss. For many children, this will be enough; they will be ready to share their thinking based on your question or scenario. Others may still need some support to kick things off. You can offer them a sentence starter or give them some time to think through their ideas or even to write about their thinking. Whether students can independently begin a conversation or still need a little help, your long-term goal is more significant: you want your young learners to be able to initiate academic conversations without the scaffolds of questions or prompts. Some strategies to support students in starting academic conversations from your prompts (as well as independently) include **presenting an idea**, **posing a question**, and **writing and drawing to plan**.

### Presenting an Idea

Throughout the year, you will likely do the majority of presenting an idea for classroom conversations. As you present ideas for students at the start of an academic conversation, share your thinking about and model the creation of the prompt to help them see why you chose that prompt. Many of your prompts are likely to be questions rather than statements. Students are likely to use presenting an idea independently more often than they will use asking a question. Because your long-term goal is for students to independently use conversations as learning opportunities, you need to work to initiate in multiple ways to help them see models for each. In addition, during a conversation you have initiated, students may opt to present an idea. When one line of thinking or inquiry has wound its way to an end, students can present an idea that is related but gets the conversation going in a new direction.

I offered my 3rd graders the following statement to discuss: "Rectangles and squares are the same thing." It was not surprising that my students were quickly agreeing and disagreeing with this idea. At the end of our discussion, I took a few moments to explain that I had chosen the prompt so that they could see how it had set up their conversation. I explained that I had opted to state an idea to them rather than ask a question, and this set them up to think about it, question it, and analyze it, rather than simply accepting it.

This is an important idea: children have been trained to accept what they are told by adults and to believe it without question. I tell my students that they can think about, question, and analyze statements others make at any time. Just because someone says something does not automatically make it true or valid. It is possible to listen to someone's statement and do exactly what they did in that conversation about squares and rectangles: think about it, discuss it.

Remember, too, that students can be on either side of this scenario. They might be the listener who decides to engage in a discussion about the other's idea, or they might be the one making the statement that is then questioned or debated by a peer. Either way, they are likely to learn something through the subsequent discussion.

## Posing a Question

Posing questions is a common conversation starter teachers choose. Questions that prompt interesting and thoughtful discussions, however, may not have a "correct" answer. In the IRE model, questions are often much more limited, with only one or few correct answers likely; the goal is for students to give an accurate response. This type of questioning is more about *checking* student learning than it is about increasing it. Questions to prompt discussion must do more than simply check students' thinking; they must push students to think more deeply, to listen to one another, to analyze what they are hearing, and to add their own thoughts.

A few years ago, one of my groups of 3rd graders had multiple discussions, all because one student asked, "If the Earth is spinning, why can't we feel it moving?" This question has answers that scientists would deem correct, but students had a lot to discuss because they didn't have a solid understanding of those answers yet. This one question, asked by a student during a science lesson, led to many thoughtful conversations in our classroom for several days.

As with offering students a statement at the beginning of a discussion and then explaining your thought process, doing so with a question can help students better understand how questions can initiate a conversation. During a study of Virginia history, I asked students, "If you had lived in colonial times, do you think you would have been a loyalist, wanted revolution, or remained neutral? Why?" This question definitely has no right or wrong answer. The discussion did get students thinking deeply about what they had learned about life in colonial Virginia. As they talked, students agreed and disagreed plenty about the choices they would have made and why they felt as they did. The reasons some students gave for their decision could be similar, for instance, whether one felt a loyalty to family back in England or a loyalty to Virginia. After the discussion, which was lively and engaging, we talked about why that question had been a good one for getting people talking.

After observing multiple discussions, I asked students to think about what makes a question good for initiating a conversation. We brainstormed some ideas and put them on a chart. These included

- The question should be interesting (we also discussed how subjective that is).
- The question should be open with lots of possibilities to discuss.
- The question should be about something others have some knowledge of or experience with, not something totally new.

After a few more discussions, we returned to this chart, checking our thoughts based on our more recent experiences and adding to the list. Eventually, I began asking students to create questions using the criteria they had listed. This offered multiple benefits.

- By creating questions about content, students demonstrated how the process supported their content-area learning.
- The practice they got in thinking through how to form a thought-provoking question helped them build that skill.
- Because my students also talked with partners and in small groups about whether their questions met the criteria and how they could improve them, they practiced their conversation skills as well.
- As one final added bonus, we used their questions to initiate many of our conversations throughout the rest of the year (taking one task off my plate).

One of the unexpected challenges, at least to me, of helping young learners initiate conversations with statements and questions was their inability to distinguish between the two. Many kindergartners and 1st graders are not always confident about what is a question and what is not. This was noticeable early in the year with my students when it came to our share time during morning meeting (see Chapter 1). The student sharing would always wrap up by saying, "I'm ready for questions and comments." My young students often said something like "I have a question. I went to Chuck E. Cheese for a birthday party, too." Distinguishing between a question and a comment was a skill they had not all mastered. To address this, when the sharer called on classmates, I would have them start their responses with either "I have a question" or "I have a comment," before saying what they wanted to say. In this way I could determine which students had a firm grasp on "question" versus "statement" and which students needed more support, depending on whether they accurately labeled what they had to say.

Sometimes, many of your students will need more help, and it is worth dedicating some whole-class time to this learning. Other times, you may want to work with the few who need your help, in small groups. Whether working on this as a whole class or in small groups, the process is the same. For a few weeks, write down all of the questions and comments from your morning meeting share. Put these on sentence strips, and with your students, sort a few at a time, separating questions and comments. Note that some students will quickly notice that questions have a question mark at the end and comments do not. If your students are unable to get past that idea, simply cut the end punctuation off the sentence strips.

After sorting a fair number of questions and comments, encourage students to identify aspects of each group. Students may notice the prevalence of questioning words such as *why*, *how*, or *what*. You can also read the sentence strips aloud together; students will notice the way voices go up at the end of questions and not at the end of comments. Some young students will get a hold of these ideas quickly; others simply need plenty of time and experience with the idea. Because both questions and statements are ways to initiate a conversation, it isn't essential for young children to be able to distinguish between them to get started.

Initiating conversations sounds fairly simple. It is something adults do on a daily basis, and frequently without a lot of thought or planning. Young children, however, are still learning how to navigate conversations—even casual conversations with friends or family members—in meaningful ways. As a result, planning for academic conversations can be an essential piece toward their success at both initiating conversations and participating in them. This planning involves thinking through what interests your students, what questions they have, and what knowledge they want to share about a given topic.

## Writing and Drawing to Plan

To help students do that thinking through and planning, you can have them write or draw. Kindergartners and 1st graders may need to draw to organize their ideas and thinking, whereas 2nd graders and older students may be able to write. These age limitations are far from set in stone; plenty of young children are ready and eager to write and many older students prefer or need, for a variety of reasons, to draw (Tomlinson, 2014). Either way, the goal is the same: for students to pause and reflect on their own thinking and understanding before jumping into a conversation.

For classes and students new to conducting academic conversations, you can begin by posing the statement or question and having students write or draw their ideas about it. This helps students prepare for the conversation to come. Initially they can take their papers with them to the conversation, but I recommend that they not do so for too long. When students have their papers in front of them, they can be distracted from the conversation and become more focused on what they want to say than on listening and responding to their peers. Some students will also see their planning page as a checklist of things they must share rather than a collection of possible ideas, which is unlikely to make for a productive or engaging academic conversation.

It won't take long for students to understand that the writing and drawing are preparation and that the ideas are still all there, in their heads, ready to share with others. After conducting some conversations with this planning, students may be ready to start discussing your statement or question without the formalized writing and drawing planning time. You may want to offer the prompt while also reminding them to take a moment and think about it before jumping in to talk with others.

You can use writing and drawing to plan as a way to move students toward initiating conversations independently by not giving them a specific prompt. For example, you might tell students,

> We've been exploring different animals' habitats and adaptations for a few weeks, and you have learned a lot about them. You may also still have some questions. Take a few moments and write or draw your ideas on this topic that you think would be useful to discuss with some of your classmates.

In book club discussions, I often give students several sticky notes. Their task, as they read the book, is to place a note on a page in the book where there is something they want to discuss. They write themselves a reminder on the note, such as "I don't understand why the main character would say that" or "I'm confused about plasma because that's not a state of matter we've talked about." They can also note something that surprised them or impressed them. The goal is for them to note things they want to discuss and write down something that could initiate a conversation. Not giving students a specific prompt opens up the topic for them and pushes them to be more thoughtful about how to initiate a conversation with others. Remember that the ultimate goal of this work is for students to be independent conversationalists, for them to not need teacher support to initiate or participate in conversations about academics.

## Introducing New Ideas

So far, I've focused on helping students learn to begin a new conversation. However, students may also use the same skills needed for getting a conversation going to introduce a new idea or question at various points in the conversation. Although a discussion may begin focused on one aspect of a topic, when that topic seems to have run its course and the conversation is slowing, we often shift slightly to another aspect of the topic. For example, when discussing why animals choose certain habitats, a student might say, "Sometimes animals, like some birds, take over another animal's habitat," or "I wonder why some animals can share a habitat and other animals have to be all by themselves." That student has just initiated a new part of the conversation.

Writing or drawing to plan for a conversation also can be helpful in showing students how to initiate in the middle of a conversation. This may happen naturally. In fact, sometimes it happens because students who do not yet have the skills to truly engage in conversation end up just throwing out their ideas and not connecting them to one another. Those students are still initiating a new part of the conversation with every new statement or question (and we will explore this more in Chapter 3, focusing on helping students learn to build on one another's thinking).

When your students engage in a conversation about an initial prompt and then someone introduces a new thought or question, this is something worth identifying. After the conversation, refer to that instance (or instances) to highlight for students what happened. This is **noticing and naming,** and it is a powerful tool. When you notice a student initiating a new idea, especially if the group seems to have exhausted the initial prompt or previous idea, take a moment and name what you saw. Following a class discussion about *Mango, Abuela, and Me* (Medina & Dominguez, 2015), I said,

> You all had so many ideas and questions about how Mia was feeling about her *abuela*. You talked a lot about that and then it got quiet for a bit. Liam noticed that, and he mentioned his idea about how Mango brought Mia and her *abuela* together. He initiated a new idea for your discussion.

Students may hesitate to introduce a new idea because they might not be sure if it is OK or what they are supposed to do. Noticing and naming this strategy shows them it's not only OK but actually helpful for moving a conversation forward, and it ensures they hear specific examples of how to do it.

> **Sentence Starters: Initiating**
>
> I'm thinking....
>
> My idea is that....
>
> I wonder....
>
> Why would...?
>
> What happens if...?

## Assessing Initiating

One of the more challenging areas to assess is students' initiating skills because you are likely to initiate the majority of the classroom conversations. One option is use a checklist to record any time a student initiates in the midst of a conversation (see Figure 2.1). I keep copies of a grid sheet with my students' names on it in alphabetical order. At the top of a column I write the skill we're practicing (or skills at the top of multiple columns), such as "Initiating" (or, if I want more specificity, "Presenting an idea and posing a question"). When I see a student use that skill, I check their name. There is some subjectivity to this, and you decide whether students get a check anytime they attempt a skill or only when they use the skill well. I may check some students' names multiple times. Others may not get a check during the same conversation. Students are going to try on and master these skills at different rates. My goal with this checklist is to have the information necessary to support students who still need some help with a skill, as well as to know when the majority of students have mastered it and we should be moving on to new skills.

FIGURE 2.1 | **SAMPLE SKILL CHECKLIST**

| Student | Introduces New Idea 10/5/20 | Asks Question to Introduce Idea 10/8/20 | Skill:_____ Date:_____ | Skill:_____ Date:_____ |
|---|---|---|---|---|
| Aalia | | ✔ | | |
| Brooklyn | | | | |
| Chloe | ✔ | ✔ | | |
| Cohen | | | | |
| D'Angelo | | | | |
| Elias | | ✔ ✔ | | |
| Fernando | | | | |
| Frankie | | – | | |
| Hayden | | | | |
| Jason | ✔ | | | |
| Jayda | | | | |
| Jh'Marri | | | | |
| Kaydra | | ✔ | | |
| Kylin | ✔ ✔ | | | |
| Mason | | | | |
| Maximo | ✔ | | | |
| Nala | | ✔ | | |
| Peyton | | | | |
| Trinity | | ✔ | | |
| Violet | | | | |

Another way to assess initiating skills is to look at your students' writing or drawing. Although your students might not use their writing or drawing to initiate a conversation, reviewing their planning will give you insight into their thinking. It is also a way to offer students feedback. You can highlight strong ideas students could use to present an idea or pose a question. You can conference with students to discuss how they might initiate a conversation using what they have written or drawn. You can even have students do the writing or drawing, submit their work to you, and delay the conversation. After reviewing their thinking, you can ask students to initiate a conversation using what they created. This approach is a powerful marriage of assessment and instruction.

## Supporting Ideas

Being able to support one's ideas in a conversation is an important skill. Offering them evidence or a defense of that thinking helps others understand it. This skill, however, is quite challenging for young learners. This is true for several reasons. One is that young children are still, naturally, quite focused on themselves. Their understanding of the world includes the idea that what they know, what they do, and what they believe are the same as everyone else. They have limited experience in the world and therefore have limited ability to recognize that others may see things differently. As a result, young children often do not defend their thinking or provide evidence because it does not occur to them to do so. They often believe that everyone else will completely agree with what they are saying. This is true despite how often young children argue with one another about everything from the best lunch option in the cafeteria to the rules for a game at recess or the best part of the newest animated movie. Such arguments do not seem to change their perception that others think and feel as they do.

Another reason that young children do not defend their thinking is because they are used to believing what they are told by others.

If you tell children that the Earth is constantly moving, they believe you, even though their own lived experiences suggest it is not true. They can't feel or see the Earth moving, but they accept that if an adult says it or if they read it in a book or see it on TV, then it is true. They trust others and expect to be trusted as well.

Young children also often jump into conversations without providing any context because they assume their listener knows what they know, has seen what they saw. If children are unable to give the context for their thinking, it is not surprising they cannot defend it.

As a result, defending their thinking or providing evidence for their thinking is something young students are unlikely to do independently. You must teach and help them develop the skills involved in supporting their thinking. There are a couple of options for helping children in this area. The first, and most basic, is **adding because**. Another, slightly more complicated strategy is **multiple sentences**.

## Adding *Because*

Students who say, "I think one-fourth is smaller than one-half," have only stated an idea; they have not defended their thinking. Simply adding *because* to the end of the statement sets them up to do so. With "I think one-fourth is smaller than one-half because I would rather have half of a candy bar than only one-fourth," they still have a long way to go in providing evidence, but the statement indicates students recognize they need to offer others in the conversation something more than an isolated idea.

Not all students will be ready to take on this strategy. For some students, simply stating their own thinking out loud in a conversation is taking a serious risk and requires a lot of effort. Eventually they will be ready to try adding *because,* but it may take awhile. Students who speak up quickly and frequently are the more significant target for this strategy. As those students take it on and use it regularly, they will model it for their more hesitant peers. Just bear in mind that not all students will be ready to do any given thing at the same time.

Although my goal is to avoid talking at all during academic conversations, this is one time I make an exception, although I try to keep it as minimal as possible. When a student (especially one who speaks up frequently) shares an idea and does not add *because,* I might jump in, "Because?" That's all I will say. This prompts the student to add *because* and explain with more detail. An added bonus, I have found, is that my students will often take on what I have modeled. When a classmate makes a statement without support, another student will frequently say, "Because?" or ask for more details. They no longer need my voice in the conversation; they are reminding each other to support their thinking.

## Using Multiple Sentences

When young children are excited about and engaged in an idea, they may have a lot to say. Just ask about their favorite video game, a recent birthday party, or a new friend! If an idea is new to them or a concept they are still working to understand, they are likely to say less. Encouraging them to use multiple sentences helps students expand their sharing. Give students the space and time to say more. Sometimes students need time to talk themselves into a deeper understanding. A student might start by saying, "I think one-fourth is smaller than one-half," then add, "Half of a candy bar is bigger than one-fourth." This student has an innate grasp of which fraction is larger, but their understanding isn't deep enough to explain. As they talk, they may work through their own thinking until they have a better understanding of why one fraction is larger—and, in the process, they will both have provided more information to their listening peers and also helped themselves gain more understanding.

This strategy may be more challenging for the others in the group than it is for the student speaking. For young students who are not naturally inclined to share multiple sentences, some silence and space to think and speak will be necessary. Others will share multiple sentences without any prompting or hesitation, but those are not the students who need help with this strategy.

Although it may feel forced or awkward to you, it may be helpful to ask your young students to say, "I'm finished," when they are ready to stop talking. Saying "I'm ready for comments and questions" after sharing during morning meeting serves this purpose. It is a signal to other students that they can have a turn. "I'm finished," in academic conversations, can accomplish the same goal. Like many other strategies, it is one that may not be needed indefinitely. Students will gain the skills to watch their classmates and listen for tells as to whether someone is finished speaking or is just pausing between multiple sentences.

> **Sentence Starters: Supporting**
>
> I think ... because ....
>
> It might be ... because ....

## Assessing Supporting

As with assessing initiating skills, you can certainly use a checklist to assess whether your students are adding *because* or sharing an idea through multiple sentences. Another option is to have your students self-assess their skills. You may not always agree with your young students' views on their progress, but you can still learn quite a bit from them. A student self-assessment can be as simple as giving them several phrases and having them choose the emoji, on a scale, that best fits their skill level or understanding. For example, you might have them respond to "I add *because* when I share my thinking" or "I often say multiple sentences about an idea when I talk." The scale could be as simple as three emojis, going from a smiling one, to a thinking one, to a frowning one. Or your scale could have four or five emojis. For older students, the scale could use words or numbers rather than emojis.

Students can also self-assess by writing about how or when they have used a specific skill. You might ask students, "When have you supported your thinking in a conversation?" or use a written prompt such as "I used supporting skills when I . . . ." If you have modeled noticing and naming, your students will have some idea regarding how to explain what they have done. Students also can set goals for growing their skill. This can be as simple as adding, "I could do better if I . . . ." to the self-assessment prompt you use. (See Figure 2.2 for an example.)

FIGURE 2.2 | **STUDENT SELF-ASSESSMENT**

| I support my thinking when I . . . |
| --- |
| *use the word because and say why I think what I think.* |

| I could do a better job of supporting my thinking by . . . |
| --- |
| *Not just agreeing or disagreeing with my friends. I can explain why I agree or disagree.* |

One of the great benefits of self-assessment is how strongly this reinforces student understanding of a skill. The more deeply students think about what they are doing (or what their classmates are doing) in conversations, the more likely they will be able to continue doing that or to take on new skills.

## Clarifying One's Thoughts

Many conversations require participants to clarify their thinking and ideas. This sometimes happens when speakers realize they are not being clear or not explaining their ideas well. Like students, many times adults begin sharing a thought and realize they are still figuring it out. Although providing evidence or defending one's thinking can help clarify what one is trying to say, it often helps to clarify meaning as well. These two ideas have definite connections. Sometimes you must clarify what you are saying because someone has asked you to do so. If a listener does not understand what you are saying, they might ask you to explain or to say more or they may simply say that they don't understand. These are signs that you need to do some clarifying. Several strategies can help young children become more skillful at clarifying their thinking: **elaborating**, **rewording or rephrasing**, and **defining**. Each of these skills can be most useful in specific situations during conversations. Students will need to learn how and when to use these skills.

The difference between these skills for clarifying thinking and the skills for supporting thinking depends on when they are needed. Supporting their thinking should be something students are frequently doing when they speak during academic conversations. It should become a norm and should be happening consistently. Clarifying is a skill used on an as-needed basis. Students might not need to clarify their thinking and sharing often, but when they do need to do so, it will be because others are not understanding them.

### Elaborating

When students are adding *because* or using multiple sentences to support their thinking, they are beginning the work of elaborating.

When elaborating, students must be able to say more than just their basic idea. As a result, elaborating—similar to the skills for supporting thinking—tends to be challenging for young children. This is a strategy students may be most likely to use when they feel they are not making themselves clear. Maybe they notice their classmates have looks of confusion on their faces. Maybe they are listening to themselves and don't feel that they are making sense. Whatever the clue might be, students will often want to elaborate their thinking while they are still speaking.

One challenge in encouraging young children to elaborate is that they will frequently repeat exactly what they said before—and sometimes they will just say it louder. Helping them see that *elaborating* means adding more and different information or details to help their listeners understand is important. Starting as early as kindergarten, students learn to add details to their writing, so it is likely they will have some familiarity with the idea of elaborating. You can use their knowledge of elaborating in writing to help them take it on in conversations.

Another thing you are likely to see happen naturally in early conversations, even with young children, is one student elaborating on what another student has said. Children want to help one another be understood and will often jump in, saying, "What she means is . . . ." This is not ideal because the student jumping in may be making many assumptions. The original speaker might not feel able to clarify the original thought if what another student said did not fully capture it. However, such instances give you an opportunity to notice and name the idea of elaboration and begin to help students take it on for themselves. For example, in my 3rd grade class's conversation about Jacqueline Woodson's *Each Kindness* (2012), my students focused on the way Maya was treated by the other girls.

 **Aikumush:** Chloe was mean, and Maya was always nice. Then she left and she didn't have a chance to say bye.

**Rameen:** Everyone in the class was mean because of how she looked, and when Chloe learned what kindness was, she felt bad. So when Maya left and Chloe didn't get to say bye and be kind, she was really sad.

Rameen took what Aikumush had said and elaborated, adding some details about it. This was a great interaction to highlight after the conversation, showing students how Rameen's additional details helped them all understand what Aikumush meant.

In lessons on elaborating, one of the things to discuss and explore together is how to tell when others listening are not understanding. One approach is to read to students from a text that is challenging for you to understand—I often use a physics textbook because that seems to be beyond my comprehension no matter how many times I read it. Tell your students that it is likely to be confusing to them because it is confusing to you. As you read, stop after a bit and have students think about how their faces look. Ask them what they notice about one another's facial expressions. You can even take pictures of them to put on a chart about elaborating, as a reminder. Ask students to identify other body language as well, such as heads shaking or turning to look at each other for clarification. If students fail to mention things that you see happening, point these out. Your goal is to help your students notice when their listeners are confused by what they are hearing.

Reread a bit of the text, stop and elaborate on it, giving more information and making it more accessible to your students. Again, have them notice how facial expressions and body language change as they begin to make sense of what they are hearing. To effectively clarify their thinking, by elaborating or by any other strategy, students need to be able to assess when their listeners need them to do so. Facial expressions and body language are typically the first feedback listeners provide to a speaker.

During a conversation that began with the prompt "Does the order of the numbers matter when you add or subtract?" I saw a student taking this skill on. Jefferson responded, "Yes, because when you add and subtract, sometimes you don't get the same answer." He paused and noticed that at least some of his classmates looked perplexed and no one was jumping in to respond to him, so he went on to give some examples. "Because 20 – 8 = 12 and 12 + 8 = 20." He was trying to elaborate on his thinking. His classmates, however, weren't quite there yet with him. He kept going: "You can do 20 – 8 = 12, but you can't do 8 – 20 = 12. You can't put the numbers in any order. It does matter." As Jefferson continued elaborating, he watched his peers, noticing when they began to look as if it was making sense, their eyes widening and their heads nodding.

## Rewording or Rephrasing

Although elaborating is a strategy most often used based on self-assessment of listeners' needs, it also works when a listener asks for clarification. Rewording or rephrasing, though, is a strategy most often used when listeners indicate they do not understand what they are hearing. It is an opportunity for the speaker to say, "What I mean is . . . ," or "What I am trying to say is . . . ." As with elaborating, young children might have difficulty with rewording or rephrasing at first, simply repeating what they previously said, word for word. The goal of rephrasing is not to simply repeat what was said, but to say it again in a different way to give listeners another opportunity to understand.

Noticing and naming is, as always, a helpful tool when students are learning to reword or rephrase. During morning meeting share time, students will often ask each other to explain something. Sometimes, students are simply confused and just say they don't understand. Because children are generally invested in what they are sharing during morning meeting, they are quick to reword or rephrase to make themselves better understood. When their turn at sharing is over, take a moment to point out why and how they did this.

As mentioned earlier in this chapter, it can be easier for students to take on new skills and strategies during conversations that are easier for them to participate in. Because they choose whether and what to share during morning meeting, students are willing to invest the time and energy to make themselves understood. That means that this part of the day is a wonderful opportunity to practice certain conversation skills. Not all skills are a good fit for the morning meeting share, though, because it isn't truly a conversation between students. It is a share followed by peers asking questions or commenting on what they heard. It does, however, help the person sharing to practice skills for sharing your thinking. Other classmates are practicing their listening and questioning skills.

## Defining

Whereas elaborating and rewording or rephrasing are helpful strategies for young learners to use to clarify their thinking, defining can be more challenging for young children and better for 2nd or 3rd graders and older. Defining requires a broader range of, and often more sophisticated, vocabulary, which makes it a more accessible strategy for upper elementary students. Defining is a more structured, rigid strategy, not as flexible when it comes to language or vocabulary, which is one of the reasons it can be so difficult. However, it is also a crucial skill for participating in conversations throughout life because it clarifies in a unique way. It directly addresses the challenge of using words, phrases, or ideas and thinking or assuming everyone means the same thing when using the same word or phrase.

Think about the times when someone said something to you, but you heard it in a very different way. Language can change over time, and words and phrases take on different meanings. In education, we see this often; even such common words as *assessment* or *proficiency* may mean different things to different people. The difficulty in finding a shared understanding for specific words can also result from cultural or linguistic differences and the different experiences students have had.

In a guided-reading group discussion of a book on weather and the Earth, several 3rd graders were sharing things they found interesting as well as what confused them as they read. They had many questions from the book and engaged in a lively discussion, listening to one another and working together to make sense of the text.

**Yaneidy** (pointing at the page about precipitation): I don't really understand what makes these things different.

**Gabriel:** Rain is water and snow and hail are frozen water.

**Luci:** Snow happens in the winter. Rain can happen anytime, except when it's really cold. Hail happens at different times too, like rain.

*As her friends tried to respond, thinking through what they knew about types of precipitation, Yaneidy got more confused.*

**Yaneidy:** No. Snow and hail. Not rain and stuff. I know about that. I'm not sure about snow and hail. I think snow and hail are both frozen. Rain isn't. So how are snow and hail different?

In this conversation, Yaneidy defined what she already understood about snow and hail, allowing her classmates to think more carefully about what she did not understand and how they could help answer her question.

If your students have not had a lot of experience defining words, they may not be ready to take on this strategy. By 2nd or 3rd grade, however, most children have some idea of what it means to define a word, so most upper elementary students should have the background knowledge and prior skills for this strategy.

You can use a couple of techniques in lessons to help students gain fluency with defining. One way is to have students think of words or phrases they use that their parents or other adults do not use. In recent years, my students have taught me about "spilling tea" and "yeeting," for example (the former means sharing gossip or telling about a secret, and the latter is tossing or throwing something). If you have listened to students' casual conversations, perhaps offer some examples—even if you do know what the words mean through hearing them in context. Brainstorm a list of words or phrases and ask students to define them for you, to explain to you what they mean. Children will be thrilled to be the experts and to teach you something new.

Another option is to practice defining words together, throughout the content you are studying. For example, in math you might create definitions for *product* and *divisor* when studying multiplication and division; in science, definitions for *vibration, compression,* and *amplitude.* Creating definitions together, with support, can be a helpful scaffold for students as they work to take on the strategy independently.

> **Sentence Starters: Clarifying**
>
> What I mean is . . . .
>
> I am trying to say that . . . .
>
> I said that because . . . .
>
> My point is . . . .

## Assessing Clarifying

Sometimes I record a conversation on a device, transcribe it, and create a conversation map. This can be fairly time-consuming and a difficult way to assess, and I do not do it for every conversation. Conversation mapping, however, provides a wealth and depth of knowledge about students' academic conversations; it captures a conversation and allows me to review and think about it more leisurely. When a conversation is happening, I know I am missing plenty of what is being said and done or how students are demonstrating skills. Much of the time I can accept that the assessment information I am collecting is not as complete as it could be. Other times, I want the most complete picture that I can possibly get. As a result, I document the conversation in some way about 20 percent of the time. Typically, I make this choice when I really want a clear picture of how well my students have mastered conversation skills. Whether I create a conversation map on the spot or record the conversation with my phone and map it later, documentation helps me to reflect more thoroughly and at leisure.

When assessing students' skills at clarifying, you are looking to see how well they are elaborating, rephrasing or rewording, and defining. These skills can be assessed with a checklist, as mentioned in Assessing Initiating, or by having students self-assess, as mentioned in Assessing Supporting. Recording the conversation, taking notes, and reviewing allows you to more closely examine what students said to determine whether they are clarifying their thinking and how well they are doing so.

Figure 2.3 is an example of notes from a conversation map I created from a class discussion. I included the date of the conversation and the prompt I posed: "What did this book teach us about friendship?" For the majority of our conversations, my students sit on the carpet in a circle so that they can all see one another. As they get seated, I write down their names, leaving room as best I can to draw lines in the middle and make notes around the outside. This conversation map shows who did not speak at all—Lindsey, Lina, Stephanie, Axel, Christian, Yaneidy, Nicky, and Daniela—as well as who spoke quite frequently: Kenia and Jefferson. One star shows where the conversation began, another where it ended, and the lines illustrate where it went from there. Aikumush got this conversation started; the lines showing who spoke from then on illustrate the conversation flow. Each dot is a new addition to the conversation, leading to the final star where Kenia wrapped things up.

FIGURE 2.3 | **EXAMPLE OF CONVERSATION MAPPING**

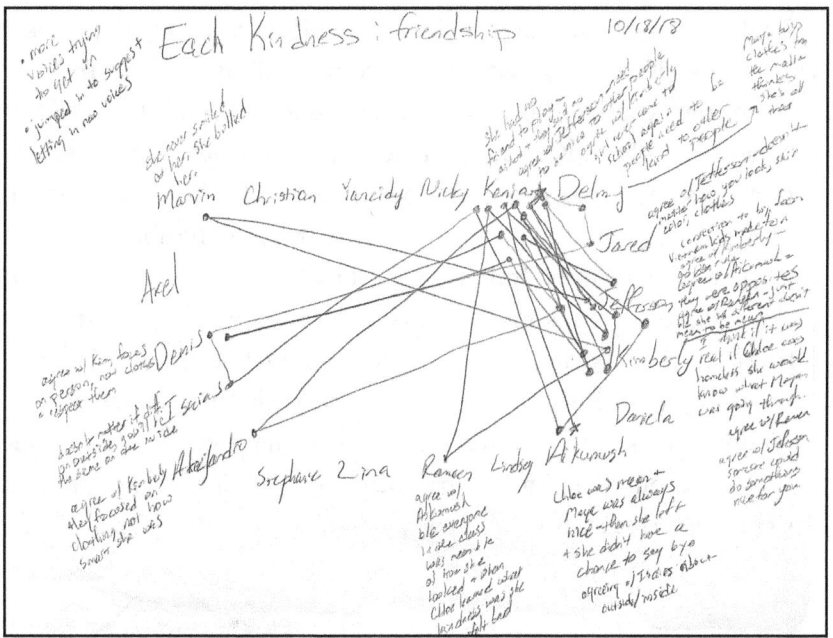

In the mapped conversation, Denis elaborates on what Kimberly said. She said, "I think if it was real, if Chloe was homeless, she would know what Maya was going through." Denis said, "I agree with Kimberly. We should focus on the person, not on the clothes, and respect them." Denis added on to Kimberly's idea, clarifying what she might have meant. Marvin said, "She never smiled at her. She bullied her." That latter sentence could be a rephrase of his first sentence, as he thought more carefully about what he was trying to say.

If we were specifically working on clarifying skills during this conversation, I would expect to see more examples of students trying on the sentence starters throughout. Because the conversation was focused more on the content than on the conversation skills, I was able to see how my students were authentically using the skills they had been practicing.

---

Students can only participate in conversations that help them learn and grow if someone gets those conversations started. In your classroom, you can do this for your students. Your students will benefit greatly, however, from becoming independent conversationalists and not needing you to start the ball rolling. In addition, engaging in such conversations is a skill they will be able to use for the rest of their lives. Initiating conversations and elaborating and clarifying their thinking are skills that will be useful in many settings for many years. As your students practice these skills, you will find them initiating conversations with their classmates at random times. Those conversations might have happened without this work, but you can be sure they will be more meaningful and significant as students gain these skills.

# 3

# EXPLORING OTHERS' THINKING

Understanding one's own thinking is not only important but also essential to understanding the thinking of others. Adults need to be able to communicate their ideas and explore those of others so that they can engage in personal, professional, and civic discourse in their daily lives. Unfortunately, most classrooms don't foster the kinds of learning experiences that help students develop this ability. Being able to explain your thinking and get your point across requires mastery of many crucial skills. If students only learn to share their thinking and not to understand others', however, they will be unable to truly engage in meaningful conversations and to grow as continuous learners independently, without the scaffolding and support of a classroom. One of the most important goals of education is to help students become independent learners, people who can continue learning and growing throughout their lives. Being able to learn from conversations with others is a significant skill they can use for years to come.

Unfortunately, classrooms typically focus on students explaining only their own thinking, rather than understanding the reasoning of others. Teachers ask questions and call on students, who respond with answers, and the teacher confirms correct answers or addresses incorrect ones. This is the IRE model (Mehan, 1979): useful for a teacher seeking to understand student thinking, identify misconceptions, and help students practice metacognition—but helping students to understand the thinking of others requires different discussion protocols far less common in the average classroom.

Think of a conversation during which you learned something new or modified your thinking. Did you agree with others in the conversation from the beginning? Did you listen closely to what they were saying and ask questions about it? Did you take some time to reflect on and analyze what you were hearing? Was the conversation engaging, or was it difficult for you to participate? (Maybe it was both!) To build new learning and understanding, students need to be able to take in new information. They can do so through conversations with others, but to do so they must have certain skills. Students need to engage in academic conversations that require meaningful back and forth, not just sharing ideas and moving on (Fisher, Frey, & Rothenberg, 2008).

To understand others, students must master an entirely different—but complementary—set of skills than that used to explain their own thinking. The skills that are crucial for students to understand the thinking of others—**listening, comprehending,** and **processing**—are complex, especially for young children. In addition, the order in which these skills are listed here might not be the order in which they would best be taught in your classroom. It may not make sense for you to teach each skill in complete isolation. For example, listening is a skill that is necessary to comprehend and process, to assess others' thinking or paraphrase. As a result, if students are showing they can do those things, it may be that noticing and naming the listening they are doing will be sufficient, and they will not need direct instruction in listening skills. Students who have had no formal instruction in conversation skills may need more support, of course. However, noticing what they are doing in casual conversations can help you plan how you respond to their specific needs. Each of these big-idea skills—listening, comprehending, and processing—can be broken down into a variety of strategies.

## Listening

The most important skill students must learn to have meaningful conversations is to truly listen to others. We have all had the experience of talking with friends or colleagues and feeling that we were not truly heard. We can see it in the person's facial expressions or the questions, or lack of questions, they ask. They may seem to be listening but are not doing so in a way that is meaningful. *Engaged listening,* listening to understand another's point of view or thinking, requires effort and skill.

In school, students are accustomed to listening so that they know what to do or *not* do (to avoid getting in trouble with a teacher); listening to understand someone else can be quite different. This is also contrary to the way students often participate in school, attempting to share their ideas and get the correct answer (i.e., the IRE model). This isn't the goal of true academic conversations, where there may not be a "correct" answer, and this shift can be difficult for many students. It is far easier to teach young children to truly listen to their peers for the sake of learning from them than it is to break older students of their habits and teach them new ways of interacting. If students have spent many years in school not seeing their peers as sources of information and ideas, only seeing teachers in that way, then this will be a difficult change to make.

Listening skills can be difficult to teach because they are less visible in many ways than other skills. There are no sentence starters for listening skills. Students have to learn to be hyper-aware of themselves, their body language, their facial expressions, and their own listening actions. As a result, although these skills are crucial for meaningful conversations, they may not be the skills to tackle first, especially with young children.

In fact, the best way to address listening skills may not be direct instruction, but rather to notice and name the things students are naturally doing as listeners during conversations to reinforce and encourage them to continue to do so and to grow those skills. Recognizing what it means to be an "active listener" will allow students to take on these skills independently. But do you want to do more than simply notice and name when students are demonstrating strong listening? Teaching students to pay attention to **physical clues**, offering students **examples and nonexamples**, and **sharing from others** will definitely help your young learners strengthen their listening skills.

## Physical Clues

Observing physical clues can be linked to the work of clarifying. In Chapter 2, we explored how to help students notice when others are confused or not understanding what they are sharing by reading facial expressions. Reading other people's facial expressions and body language is crucial during conversations. For listening skills, the focus is more on noticing one's own body language rather than that of others. This includes making eye contact, facing the person who is speaking, and controlling facial expressions and body language.

Students will make progress more quickly in any given skill, such as truly listening to one another, when they have the opportunity to focus on that skill alone. Keeping the cognitive load focused only on improving as listeners—rather than on improving as listeners and also mastering some other conversation skills or content—is key. As students become more comfortable using their active listening skills and monitoring themselves in doing so, you can raise the cognitive load. Don't underestimate the work students will need to do to strengthen their listening skills. Take the time to develop this, and it will pay off in future conversations.

Noticing and naming the physical clues that demonstrate strong listening skills is something that you gradually introduce to students. You might say, "I noticed D'Jori was always looking at whoever was talking. Sometimes she was nodding her head as others were speaking. I could see she was listening carefully." In addition to the many opportunities that you have to notice and name students' actions in the classroom, you can use photos—either of students in the classroom or of others—and video clips for group noticing-and-naming listening actions. It can be great fun for students to look at photos or short video clips from their favorite movies or television shows and identify whether characters are listening or not based on the physical clues. One word of warning: animated movies and shows don't work as well as those with actual people.

Based on your noticing and naming, you can begin to develop with your students a list of what it looks like to be an active listener: making eye contact with the person talking, turning your body to face the person, nodding, or furrowing one's brow in confusion. Ideally, students will be able to share at least some of these attributes of an active listener. Creating a chart together, based on what they are noticing their peers do when they are listening, will help students remember and practice the skills. You can include photos of your students on the chart as an additional reminder.

## Examples and Nonexamples

As you have been noticing and naming, students have seen many examples of strong listening. Nonexamples can be equally important. Acting out nonexamples is fun and can get silly, but it also can help students remember what it feels like to be distracted or other nonlistening actions. You and another teacher, or you and a student, can role-play a conversation. One person can model the examples and the other can model nonexamples. Young children will find it hilarious to watch a teacher behave badly: ignoring the other person, looking around them, messing with things, talking over them, possibly even walking away. How extreme you make your nonexamples depends on how likely you think your students are to need reminders not to do certain things. You want them to see the behaviors they might demonstrate that would be distracting to themselves or others. After this demonstration, students can make a list of the listening skills and the distracted behaviors. I guarantee it is a lesson that will stick with your students.

Upper elementary students can also look at images from media (e.g., TV shows or movies, political debates, business meetings) and discuss whether they think the people in the pictures are listening to one another. Explaining why they think "yes" or "no" will help them notice more clearly the things serious listeners do. You can collect such images, and you can also ask students to look for examples in real life that demonstrate listening and ones that demonstrate not listening. Through this assignment, your students will find images that will be relevant to themselves and their classmates. Not only will the relevance be powerful, but also having students on the hunt for images will deepen their thinking about what listening means and looks like.

## Sharing from Others

When students engage in classroom conversations, with a partner or small group, teachers often ask them to share at the end. Typically, students share something they were thinking and mentioned in the discussion. To practice listening skills, make one small change. Ask students to *share from others*: instead of sharing something they contributed to the conversation, they share something they heard from a classmate.

To begin, have students talk with a partner about their weekend or activities outside school. Chapter 2 explored balancing the cognitive load; here, you are starting with a comfortable conversation topic. After pairs have talked, ask students to share with the larger group something they learned from their partners. Having students share their partner's information rather than their own requires them to listen carefully to what they are being told. Discussing something personal in a more social, less formal conversation allows students to focus on their listening skills without the high-cognitive load of needing to understand something new.

As students grow their listening skills, you can introduce "turn and talks" (West & Cameron, 2013) about student learning and content knowledge (in pairs or small groups) and have students share something another student said, rather than their own thinking. This is slightly more challenging and raises the cognitive load because this is not a strictly social conversation. During conversations about their lives, students can focus on their listening skills without the additional focus on academic content. This strategy pushes students to do both at the same time.

## Assessing Listening

As you are noticing and naming students' listening strengths, you are informally assessing them. You are identifying which students are using listening skills—and *which* listening skills—well. You can easily add a more formal component to this with a checklist. In my classroom, a clipboard with blank checklists (with my students' names) is always at the ready. I can quickly grab it to make notes on whatever comes up. For example, I made column headings of the listening skills we were working on: Looking at the Person Speaking, Turning to Face the Speaker, Facial Expressions (I was looking for wide eyes or furrowed brows but was open to whatever I might notice that showed a student was actively listening), and Nodding in Agreement. It is impossible to watch every student in the classroom at once with the level of observation required for accurate assessment. I opted to watch three or four students at a time for a period of three to five minutes. I could keep a focus on that many students, and that length of time gave me a pretty good amount of data for each student. A checklist like this not only allows me to identify individual students who need more support to develop specific skills, but also makes it easy to see if there is a skill that few to none are taking on yet.

In Chapter 2, we explored the idea of self-assessment by students. For assessing listening skills, another option is peer assessment. This is an especially good choice when students are talking in pairs. Each student can assess how well their partner was listening to them—perhaps on a checklist similar to yours, which allows them to indicate anything they notice their partner doing. Or it could look more like a scaled self-assessment, allowing them to rate how well their partner was looking at them, facing them, and sharing out what they had said. These assessments from the person who is speaking can tell you a lot. As an added bonus, working through this assessment reinforces the student's knowledge and understanding of the various listening skills.

## Comprehending

Once your students are actively listening to their peers during conversations, they are ready to move on to checking that they are comprehending what they are hearing. Think about your own experience engaging in conversations: you make frequent assumptions about what others are saying, based not only on the deep, engaged listening you are doing but also on your own background knowledge and understanding of the context of the conversation. Listeners bring a lot to the table that may or may not be accurate. Checking for comprehension, checking to be sure one is accurately understanding others, is crucial for making meaning. This process has several steps that come naturally and almost simultaneously to most adults: listening carefully, reflecting on what they are hearing, and processing what they grasp of it.

Academic conversations in classrooms suffer from the same pitfalls as social conversations in other settings. Students bring their knowledge of the content—including any questions or misconceptions they may have—to the conversation and to what they are hearing. If they do not take the time to check their comprehension of their peers' ideas, students may reinforce misconceptions or even form new ones. The goal of academic conversations is to help students better and more deeply understand the ideas and content they are studying, so it is crucial for them to be confident and correct in what they are hearing and comprehending.

Several strategies can be taught even to the youngest learners to help them take responsibility for checking their comprehension. **Asking questions** is one that feels most natural for many children. Two big reasons for asking questions are (1) to gain more information and (2) to clarify comprehension—which is a stepping-stone toward paraphrasing. **Paraphrasing** is a more advanced, complex skill that may be a better fit as students get a little older, possibly in grades 3 and up.

## Asking Questions for Information

Asking questions because you are not certain about what someone else is sharing is a risk. It requires you to let others know that you are not confident in your knowledge. The work described in Chapter 1 about moving mindsets and developing a classroom environment that encourages and welcomes risk taking is an important foundation. Students will not only be able to ask such questions and admit uncertainty, but also be open to the possibility that they may have misconceptions or gaps in their knowledge and skills. That openness is an important first step in learning something new. Because of the risk involved in this strategy, teacher modeling and noticing and naming are two of the most powerful ways to help students take it on.

Asking questions to gain more information about what one is hearing is only possible if students are listening carefully as well as considering what they are hearing. Such questions could be as simple as saying, "Can you explain that again?" or "I don't understand what you mean. Can you tell me more?" One of the first steps in teaching students this skill is for you to model such questioning on a regular basis. Students often share information from their lives or talk about their learning without a lot of context, especially young students. They make assumptions that the listener has the background knowledge to follow what they are sharing. When it comes to content learning—something everyone is working on together—this is frequently true. It may not be as likely with their personal experiences. I have had many conversations with excited primary students who want to tell me all about something they did, away from school.

**Diego:** Yesterday my mom took us to play games and we had so much fun!

**Me:** Wow! That sounds exciting. I'm not sure I totally understand, though. Where did your mom take you? Who else went with you? What games did you play?

Knowing Diego well, I could infer that his mother took him and his siblings to Dave & Buster's and engage in a discussion with him. But inference requires the listener to make some leaps. Even given my knowledge of Diego and the things he likes to do, though, I instead used this opportunity to model asking questions to understand. This approach not only helps students gain the language to ask clarifying questions on their own, but also shows them that it is not a problem or a weakness to not understand someone else. Everyone has times when they do not understand, including adults and teachers.

This is true for content-area learning as well. For example, a student might say, "I am really confused about those issues with the Church. Why did the king want to change things?" If your class is studying Henry VIII, you would likely be able to hold a conversation with this student without any clarification. Even knowing the context, however, it might better serve the student if you reply, "I'm not sure what you are asking me. Which king? What issues are confusing you?" Asking for more information is respectful and necessary if one wants to learn from others. Teachers can model asking questions on a daily basis, both informally and about academic topics. It requires rethinking and retraining how you engage with students; the natural inclination is often to make the inference and move forward, but this approach will show benefits if done deliberately.

Noticing and naming when students are asking questions to build their confidence in what they are doing is another crucial strategy. Many essential conversation skills are things students do quite naturally but do not realize they are doing until you highlight these skills. Helping students be aware of the conversation skills they are using will help them use those skills more deliberately. Asking for help or asking questions to understand requires students take a risk and admit what they don't know—that is something to identify and to celebrate. Recognizing when students take risks and pointing it out as a worthy thing to do is one way to continue fostering an atmosphere of trust and community.

During or at the end of a conversation, point out students who did this. For example, "I noticed Josue told Ashley he didn't understand what she was saying and asked her to explain it more. That showed he was listening to her and he wanted to understand what she was saying." Naming the behavior and its effect also helps other students recognize language their peers are using that they too can use in the future to ask questions.

Like modeling, noticing and naming requires watching for teaching opportunities. It can be done in carefully planned lessons but will be even more beneficial if done at every opportunity, every time you see a student using questions to check their grasp of what someone else is saying. This is especially true if the noticing and naming is shared with a larger group of students than just the two or few engaging in the conversation.

## Asking Questions for Clarification

The other purpose for questioning is to clarify. This might look like asking, "Are you saying. . . ?" Asking questions for clarification presumes some understanding on the part of the questioner and thus requires slightly less risk than asking questions for information. Both types of questioning, however, require the same listening skills and processing of one's own thinking about another's ideas—possibly even more. Questions that clarify understanding are built on what the listener has understood of the ideas being shared and what might still be unclear. Such questions require the listener to think about what they are hearing as well as what they already know or think they know. The listener might say, "I understand that you noticed a theme of facing challenges in the story, but can you say more about what you read that showed you that?" Questions for clarification are often more specific than questions for information.

As with other skills, teachers can model, as well as notice and name, asking questions for clarification to great effect. This is especially true when working with younger students. In the following conversation, students were in a reading group discussing *Our World of Wonders* (Canetti, 1999).

**Aikumush:** Why did they build the castle?

**Rameen:** Maybe they built it for kings and queens.

**Lina:** Yeah, maybe for kings and queens. That's usually what castles are for.

**Aikumush:** But then why does it look so old? If kings and queens live there, why would it look so old?

In this conversation, I can notice and name how Aikumush asked questions for clarification. What she is reading and hearing from her classmates about this castle is not fitting with her prior knowledge. I can point out to her and the others how she is working to understand by continuing to ask questions.

Older students can do some writing and work in small groups to help one another more strongly develop their skills of asking questions for clarification. Pausing a conversation and having students write down what they have heard and what they understand helps students slow down their thinking process. It breaks into pieces the listening, reflecting, and processing to help students do each step carefully and with more awareness, and it will help them take on the steps more independently and fluidly over time. After writing, students can return to the conversation and begin with any questions for clarification they may have identified a need to ask.

Or, in groups of three students each (keeping the cognitive load in mind), two of the students engage in a conversation and the third observes and analyzes the conversation. When first implementing this approach, you might keep conversations social and informal; students are just beginning to develop their skills of asking questions for clarification, and you can move to more academic conversations as they grow stronger. The role of the third student will be dependent on the level of questioning skill shown by the other two. If the two students conversing are using questions to clarify well, the third student is there to notice and name. This activity is especially helpful when some students are taking this strategy on while others are struggling. This grouping offers students who may be having trouble with this skill ample opportunities to hear strong questioning language used in context and then highlighted by another student. It will reinforce examples they can try.

On the other hand, if students are having difficulty using this strategy independently, the role of the third student in the group is more complex. That student must listen carefully to the conversation to identify misconceptions or times where one student or the other would have benefited from questioning. The student can make a note or can immediately pause the conversation to point out the opportunity. The three students could then work together to brainstorm language that would have helped clarify for the listener.

Writing and this type of small-group work are sophisticated strategies to help students gain and grow skills for asking questions for clarification. Younger students could pause the conversation and draw or silently reflect on what they've heard rather than write, or work in a small group that includes a teacher or older student to help guide their learning.

**Me:** How are 2-D and 3-D shapes related?

**Diego:** They are the same because they are both shapes.

**Kristopher:** 3-D shapes, like a cube, have squares in it.

**Josue:** What was that, Kristopher?

**Kristopher:** They're related because they have some of the same shapes in them.

**Jeremy:** And they're related because they both have vertices, faces, and stuff like that.

**Ariany:** I agree with Kristopher. A 2-D shape can make a 3-D shape.

**Vy:** Ariany, are you saying a cube is related to a square because it has a square in it?

**Ariany:** Yes.

**Kristopher:** What if there are other shapes?

**Josue:** Are you saying there are other kinds of shapes we don't know?

**Kristopher:** Maybe.

In this conversation, after my initial question, students asked questions for various reasons as they explored their understanding of 2-D and 3-D shapes. Josue asked a question for information from Kristopher, Vy asked a question to clarify that she understood what Ariany was saying, and Kristopher asked a question that added a whole new dimension to the conversation.

## Paraphrasing

As with asking questions for clarification, paraphrasing is based on a presumption of understanding. Listeners frequently make assumptions about what others actually mean. Although they may be correct most of the time, when they are wrong, it can cause problems. Paraphrasing what you are hearing helps ensure that you understand—and it can also help the speaker because, upon hearing their thoughts paraphrased, they may realize they did not say what they intended to say or did not complete their thinking.

Paraphrasing can be a challenge for many students because it often feels unnecessary to them. Their confidence in their own grasp of what others have said is strong and can make paraphrasing seem extraneous. Of course, that is the purpose of paraphrasing: to confirm or validate one's understanding.

**Vy:** So you are saying that animal habitats are being changed by climate change and that is hurting the animals, which will eventually cause hurt to us as well?

**Naomi:** Yes, and that climate change is hurting the animals' habitats because of what we are doing. So really we are hurting ourselves.

Vy believed she had all of the information and a clear grasp of what Naomi was sharing but was actually missing a crucial piece.

Paraphrasing can be an easier skill to teach younger children while also being sophisticated and useful for upper elementary students. The strategies of showing students examples and nonexamples and using **structured practice** can help them identify paraphrasing and begin taking on the language.

Offering students examples and nonexamples can be done orally or in writing. Young children who are still developing independent reading skills will need to do this activity with audio or video recordings or live presentations. Students who are able to read independently can look at textual examples and nonexamples. Bearing in mind the need to balance the cognitive load, begin with topics familiar to students. You should offer strong, brief, and unambiguous examples of paraphrasing and clear nonexamples. For example, a text or recording could have three or four sentences about a popular movie, followed by a brief paraphrase or a statement that is off-topic or includes confusion. Figure 3.1 highlights an example of paraphrasing using the movie *Moana*. Students can decide together if the second statement is an accurate paraphrase or not. They should be able to identify some strengths in the paraphrase while noticing that the final sentence goes off topic from the original statement.

A crucial part of this activity is having students explain how they know whether the example is a paraphrase or not. For the students who quickly know, that may not seem important, but for those who

## FIGURE 3.1 | SAMPLE PARAPHRASE WITH EXAMPLES AND NONEXAMPLES

**Synopsis**
In the movie *Moana,* the title character is a young girl living in Polynesia. Her father is the chief of the tribe on the island where they live. Moana, however, dreams of something bigger and wants desperately to travel away from the island, across the sea. This is not allowed in her tribe. The fishermen in her tribe are unable to catch any fish, and Moana learns that the demigod, Maui, caused this trouble and he must return the heart of Te Fiti to resolve it. Moana sets out to find Maui and to make things right.

**Paraphrase**
*Moana* is a movie about a girl who wants to save her island. They can't get any more fish and she needs to find the demigod, Maui, to fix that problem. Moana must leave the island, which has long been forbidden, in order to do this. It's a lot like other movies with kids who want to save the world.

are working hard to identify, having the explanation will help them in the future. The examples from this activity can also serve as a place to begin creating an anchor chart with language or sentence starters for paraphrasing. As students gain paraphrasing skills, they can even create their own examples and nonexamples for their classmates to identify.

Structured practice requires students to take on paraphrasing skills in a conversation. One of the easiest ways to set this up in a classroom is to make two circles of students, one circle inside the other. The two circles should sit facing each other so that each student has a partner for the conversation. Give the students a topic to discuss, social or academic, and have students in the outside circle talk to their partner for a minute or two. Then ask those in the inside circle to paraphrase what they heard. Students can use language from the class anchor charts or sentence starters to help them. As students engage in these structured practice conversations, listen in to notice and name strong paraphrasing language. After a conversation or two, one circle can move clockwise and give everyone a new partner. With a new topic, the paraphrasing structured practice can continue.

> **Sentence Starters: Comprehending**
>
> I don't understand. Can you explain that again?
>
> Can someone else explain what _____ is saying?
>
> Could you say that in another way?
>
> Can you give me another example?
>
> Can you tell me more about that?
>
> Do you mean . . . ?
>
> Can you say more about . . . ?
>
> I hear you saying . . . .
>
> It sounds to me like you are saying . . . .
>
> Let me see if I've got this right: You are saying . . . .

## Assessing Comprehending

Because it can be difficult to get inside your students' heads and assess how well they are comprehending what they are hearing, these skills are ideal for student self-assessment. Figures 3.2 and 3.3 provide examples of student self-assessments. Figure 3.2 provides a quick check-in, allowing students to indicate how confident they feel in their ability to do each thing on the list. Figure 3.3 gives them an opportunity to identify the behaviors that demonstrate their use of the skill. Note that the wording of the statements is student-friendly and age-appropriate for elementary students. Figure 3.2 is more appropriate for younger students, in kindergarten and 1st grade. Figure 3.3 requires students be able to write about their skills, so it's a more appropriate tool for later in 1st grade or above. The repetition in the phrases is designed to help students focus on the "why"—the reason for using their comprehending skills.

FIGURE 3.2 | **STUDENT SELF-ASSESSMENT A: COMPREHENDING**

| I Statements | | | |
|---|---|---|---|
| I ask questions when I need more information. | | | |
| I ask questions to be sure I understand what someone else is saying. | | | |
| I paraphrase to make sure I understand what someone else is saying. | | | |

FIGURE 3.3 | **STUDENT SELF-ASSESSMENT B: COMPREHENDING**

| I Statements | I use these skills when . . . |
|---|---|
| I ask questions when I need more information. | |
| I ask questions to be sure I understand what someone else is saying. | |
| I paraphrase to make sure I understand what someone else is saying. | |

## Processing

Once students are listening well and are certain they truly comprehend what they are hearing, they will need to process it. Processing requires reflection and analysis of what they have heard. Making meaning of what one reads or hears requires processing and reflection. Without this step, students simply take in information without taking it on. Processing and reflecting on what they have listened to and comprehended is the point at which they fit this new information into what they already knew, building new knowledge, and the point at which they question and analyze for validity.

Many students learn early that they should simply accept what they are told in school or from adults as true, just as they should believe what they read in books. Assessing ideas critically and processing them is not something students are often taught, at least not until they are older. In many early elementary state standards, students are expected to listen, participate in conversations, ask questions, and retell what they are hearing; they are not expected to analyze or deeply process what they hear. The Common Core State Standards in English language arts (National Governors Association Center for Best Practices, Council of Chief State School Officers, 2010) require students in 5th grade to "review the key ideas expressed and draw conclusions in light of information and knowledge gained from the discussions." Seventh graders in Texas (Texas Education Agency, 2010) are expected to "draw conclusions about the speaker's message." In Virginia, where I teach, 9th graders "evaluate impact, purpose, point of view, reasoning, and use of evidence and rhetoric" (Board of Education, Commonwealth of Virginia, 2002). Taking conversation ideas beyond listening and participation are considered skills beyond young children's capabilities.

Processing what one is hearing is a difficult and complex, but crucial, skill. It is one that will help students build and grow from a young age. Toddlers are certainly capable of processing what they are hearing, as can be seen from the myriad questions they ask during conversations. It is a disservice to young children to expect them to listen and participate but not to process and question. The strategies students in K–2 might use for processing can be different from those taught to students in grades 3–5. However, which strategies are most needed will depend greatly on the extent of experience students have with participating in meaningful academic conversations. Students can begin with **agreeing and disagreeing** and continue with **adding on**.

## Agreeing and Disagreeing

For the youngest students, agreeing or disagreeing is one way to begin processing what they are hearing. Most children will have plenty of experience agreeing or disagreeing with siblings and parents and will feel confident taking on this strategy in classroom conversations. Doing so, however, requires that students have taken the time to explore the ideas they are hearing. They must have listened carefully and ensured their own comprehension to determine if they agree or disagree. In a classroom conversation, a student's agreement or disagreement may seem to an adult like a simple statement, but it is a sign of the conversational work they are doing.

For some students, simply stating "I agree" or "I disagree" may be sufficient for this skill, at least at first. It is a way into the conversation for students who might otherwise be hesitant to speak up. You may want to note such comments so that you can celebrate students on their engagement. It's also helpful to follow up after the discussion to better understand and get more information about their thinking because simple agreement or disagreement does not provide much insight. Another option is to have such students write about their thinking after the discussion.

Initially, it can be important to notice and name when students agree or disagree with others, to highlight the listening they are doing. One cannot agree or disagree without listening to what another person is saying. It is also important to highlight when students say more in these moments; this will help the class recognize the value in explaining why they agree or disagree. If you have sentence starters that say "I agree with \_\_\_\_" and "I respectfully disagree with \_\_\_\_," you can add the word *because* to them as students take it on.

Students will likely quickly use agreeing and disagreeing in conversations. Helping them recognize what they are doing—beyond the listening and comprehending—will come eventually. When students are confidently listening and agreeing and disagreeing with others, it's time to have a conversation about their thinking. Help students see that when they agree or disagree, they are thinking critically about what they are hearing. Knowing they can disagree gives students the power to listen critically and not to accept blindly. They are not just taking in information as they listen; they are thinking about it and questioning what they think about it.

One way to help this process is to give students a statement with which they can agree or disagree. If the statement is a true one, such as "Squares are a special kind of rectangle," students will probably not gain the same understanding of what they are doing when they disagree as they will if the statement is untrue. Offering them the statement "Shapes with the same perimeter will have the same area" will better serve the purpose. When the discussion revolves around *why* the statement might be untrue, you have the opportunity to point out to students that they proved something that you told them was wrong. This will help them to see that statements from adults, teachers, books, websites, and other authorities are not always accurate and are worth questioning.

## Adding On

As students become proficient with agreement and disagreement, they will be ready to process what they are hearing and share in a way that adds on. This is a more complex strategy and may be more appropriate for students in grades 3–5. Agreeing and disagreeing requires students to process what they are hearing for themselves. Adding on not only includes that internal processing but also moves the learning forward by sharing new thinking on the idea being discussed.

Teaching this skill can be challenging because it is one of the most complex things you are asking students to do in conversation. They must listen carefully, comprehend what they are hearing, process it and make meaning for themselves, and then explain their own thinking. That's a lot of layers happening in the midst of a conversation.

To begin, break the process apart. You can use structured practice, as you did for paraphrasing, with some modifications. As students face a partner for a conversation, give them a statement with which to agree or disagree. For example, *"Light* and *fire* are synonyms." Allow students some time for quiet reflection to determine if they agree or disagree. It can be helpful to provide them with a sentence starter (*"I disagree that* they are synonyms *because I think that . . ."*). Taking ideas in isolation lowers the cognitive load and allows students to focus on how they can add on without needing to follow an entire conversation.

In a classroom conversation about Minh Lê and Dan Santat's *Drawn Together* (2018), my students shared these thoughts.

**Aikumush:** Grandpa was really quiet in the book. Maybe he was lonely.

**Alex:** Why was the grandfather lonely?

**Trinity:** I agree with Aikumush. That grandpa . . . he didn't really talk much.

**Elle:** Yeah, why were they shy when they were at home alone?

**Jordan:** I disagree with Elle because I didn't think they were shy. They just speak different languages.

**Kylee:** I think he was using another language.

**Gavin:** I agree with Kylee. The kid is talking English and the grandpa isn't.

**Jordan:** I agree with Gavin. The language looked like Japanese or Chinese.

In this conversation, agreeing and disagreeing is a skill my students definitely had down. And they aren't just agreeing or disagreeing; they are adding on their own thoughts to what their classmates shared. For example, Jordan disagreed, he added *because*, and then he added on his own thinking. With practice, young students will bring together all of these skills and engage in conversations that will push their own thinking and the thinking of their friends.

**Sentence Starters: Processing**

I agree with _____ because . . . .

I respectfully disagree with _____ because . . . .

I disagree about _____ because I think that . . . .

Despite disagreeing with _____ about this idea, I agree about . . . .

_____'s point about this idea was important because . . . .

I see it differently because . . . .

My idea is slightly different . . . .

It is important to remember that not everything students share in academic conversations will be accurate. Their agreements and disagreements and their additions will highlight confusions and misconceptions in their understanding. Sometimes other students will correct those confusions or misconceptions, and sometimes they will not. (We'll discuss options and strategies for addressing instructional, content-area concerns in Chapter 6.)

## Assessing Processing

It can be difficult to truly assess how well students are processing a conversation; assessing how well they are agreeing and disagreeing or adding on is definitely easier. As discussed in Chapter 2, documenting a conversation in some way will help you look more closely at how well students are using those skills.

In the conversation mapped in Figure 3.4, I can see that Josue is agreeing frequently. I also notice that he does not seem to be explaining his thinking when he does so. He said, "I agree with Vy" then "I agree with Angelina" and then "I agree with Vy." Some processing is clearly happening as he listens, but he may not be comprehending as deeply as possible. Ashley is also agreeing, but she added on some of her own thinking about what has been said: "I agree with Josue about multiplication and division. I still find those hard." Josue had said he found multiplication and division hard when he started them.

This conversation does not give me a lot of assessment data about my students' processing skills. One reason for this, I believe, is that the cognitive load on the topic for this conversation was high. I asked students, "What makes math challenging for you?" My goal here was focused on their thinking about math, not on their conversation skills. It is a good reminder to me, however, that *every conversation offers insight into students' thinking*, about both the topic at hand and their skills in discussion.

**FIGURE 3.4 | CONVERSATION MAP: ASSESSING PROCESSING**

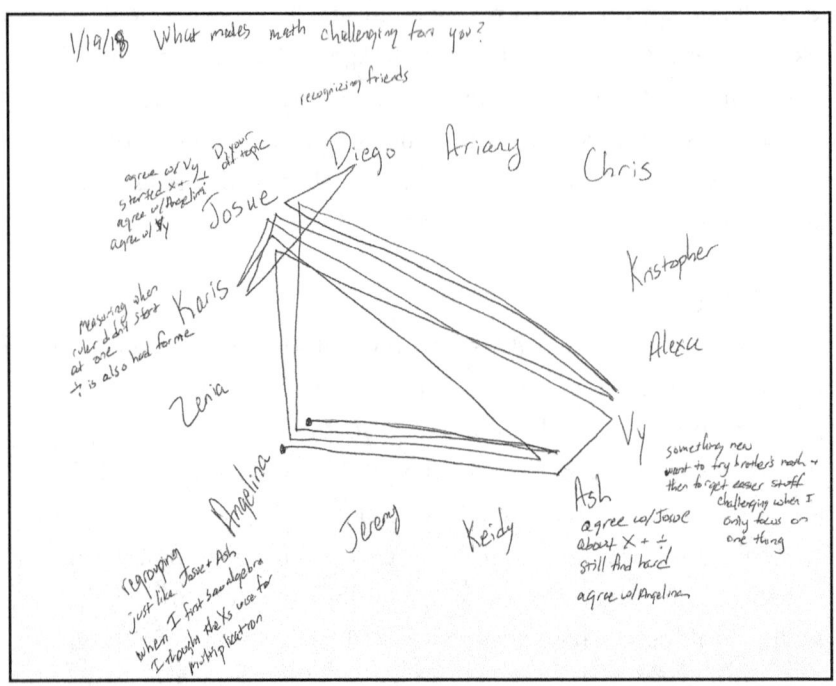

Learning to listen deeply, comprehend what you are hearing, and process your own thinking about the information are difficult but crucial skills. Students who practice such conversations in classrooms will be far better prepared to engage in discourse throughout their lives, personally and professionally (Spies & Xu, 2018). They will also be able to grow the skills they need to synthesize and co-create meaning with others through conversations, building new knowledge together. Take a moment and think about how powerful that is. Think about the lifelong skills your young students are gaining and what that will mean for them in relationships and communities.

# 4

# SYNTHESIZING THINKING

The immense amount of work you and your students have done—to improve their skills at sharing their own thinking and ideas and at exploring and understanding the ideas and thinking of others—is all a part of working toward synthesizing thinking. Taking all of their own thinking and bringing it together with what they are learning from others and developing new and deeper understanding is the ultimate goal. Through synthesizing and co-creating ideas, students gain new knowledge.

In some ways, the skills students can practice for synthesizing thinking will feel like adding building blocks to the foundation you have built through the previous skills. These new skills will be natural ongoing growth, a continuation of the work you've been doing together. In other ways, these skills will be extremely challenging. The work of synthesizing thinking involves a lot of metacognition and can be difficult to model, explain, and identify. Be willing to take your time and expect that this may not happen quickly—but know that *it will happen*. Even the youngest learners will synthesize thinking in conversations, although this may look different for different students.

Sharing one's own thinking can be a monologue or a one-way street. Chapter 3 started the work of developing two-way conversational skills. Trying to understand another's thinking leads to genuine conversation that requires multiple participants. This chapter takes it to another level. Combining one's own ideas and thoughts with those of multiple people and using these to build new knowledge and understanding is not just a two-way street but a complex set of intersections and traffic circles. As a result, it can get your learners a lot further.

To kick off the skills needed for synthesizing thinking, we'll start with **staying on topic** and the related idea of **getting back on topic.** Any conversation can easily follow a tangent (and sometimes that can be quite helpful); it's important to be able to identify when that happens and refocus the talk. Once their conversations are staying focused, your students can work on **connecting ideas.** So much of learning is about making connections between diverse topics, ideas, and questions. Helping students learn to connect ideas they hear and think about during conversations is a skill that will transfer to much of their other learning.

One last skill we'll explore in this chapter is **including others.** Students who are learning together will soon recognize the value of hearing from their peers. Noticing who has not spoken in a conversation, for whatever reason, and asking for their thoughts is not only respectful but also beneficial to everyone.

## Staying on Topic

Take some time to notice how you use these skills yourself. (This applies to all of the skills in this book, but especially the ones in this chapter.) What does it sound like when you're in a conversation and you begin to bring ideas together? What are you thinking when conversations begin to get off track? What do you do? It can be difficult to teach skills that you do naturally because it is hard to break things apart and see their components. Slowing down and noticing how you stay on topic in your own conversations will help you to teach it to young children.

- Do you notice yourself following a tangent, or does it help to have someone else redirect you?
- How do you feel when you notice a conversation is moving away from its topic?
- What clues let you know a conversation is straying? What do you say to help refocus a conversation? What specific language do you use?
- How do you feel when you make a connection between your thinking and someone else's?
- How do you respond to connecting your thinking to another's? Do you jump in and talk over them? Do you need some time to process that connection?
- What happens when someone else makes a connection to your thinking? How do you respond?
- How do you know when you have connected ideas? What alerts you in your mind or body?

Another thing to keep in mind, when planning to support students as they develop the skills described in this chapter, is that these are tough skills to master. They are often tough for adults, and they are definitely tough for young children. Think back to the idea of balancing the cognitive load (Chapter 2). It may be worthwhile to plan for some informal, nonacademic conversations early in the year to enable focusing on these skills. (Later in the year this can seem difficult as you feel the pressure of the planning and pacing guide and curriculum.)

Consider the topics you hear students discussing at recess or before school and identify some possibilities for conversations that will help your students really think about practicing these skills while not needing to also think hard about the content. Topics that I have found to be popular with many young students include video games (even those who aren't actively playing are generally quite familiar with the games), new movies or TV shows, recent events at school or in the community (e.g., a spirit week, evening event), and holidays. The goal is to find something that will connect with many of your students and a topic that is comfortable for them.

For young children, staying on topic in any conversation can be challenging. If you've ever had the opportunity to eavesdrop on a bunch of 1st or 2nd graders chatting among themselves at lunch or recess, you know how meandering their conversation can be and how it can jump in quite unexpected ways. This rarely seems to bother young children; they adapt and connect quickly to new directions in the discussion or push it back if the previous topic was important to them. Conversations are typically allowed to flow according to the will of the participants. This tends to be true for adults as well. You may be more aware of this when a conversation is moving in a new direction, but normally it's simply how conversations work.

Academic conversations require a bit more focus on the part of students. This is also true for the more important conversations in our adult lives. When talking with family members about important decisions or future plans, it's essential to focus on the issues at hand and not go off in an unexpected direction. Being able to recognize when a conversation is straying or has strayed off track and to keep or get it back on track are crucial skills for meaningful conversations. These are also skills that require some level of collaboration between those engaged in the talk. To help students keep conversations on topic, both teachers and students need to work on several skills: **building self-awareness, noticing a move off topic,** and **getting back on topic.**

A goal of academic conversations is to have students reach new learning. Earlier in this chapter, I mentioned conversations that can be one-way or two-way streets. When traveling somewhere new, one might turn and wind through cities and countryside, while always moving forward and aiming for a destination. Learning is rarely a straight line. It requires some turning and winding to get somewhere new. In an effective conversation, all participants are aiming for a destination. It's far more complicated to get past the monologues of sharing one's own thinking and on the two-way street of understanding someone else, and it requires more work from everyone to keep moving forward.

## Building Self-Awareness

The first step in staying on topic is mastering self-awareness and self-management, two of the CASEL (2021b) competencies. *Self-awareness* involves recognizing one's own emotions and thoughts. You can't make sure you're focused on the topic at hand unless you are consciously monitoring your own thinking. *Self-management* involves impulse control and self-discipline to remain focused on the topic, even when you find your thoughts straying elsewhere. Keeping on topic can be challenging for young learners. Thinking about the social-emotional competencies involved can help you understand all the work that your students must do to manage this.

Keeping on topic is challenging to teach children because it is deeply metacognitive, requiring a strong awareness of their own thought processes. Helping young children learn to monitor their own thinking will help them be successful far beyond academic conversations. Your school's counselor is one resource to help you with strategies for deepening students' awareness of their thinking.

School counselors do a lot of work helping students develop stronger social-emotional skills and therefore might have some great tips or advice for strategies you can use. In addition, they might also have lessons they regularly teach students in your grade level or younger that you can refer to and build on.

Books or games such as "Where's Waldo?" and "I Spy" help students practice impulse control and build stamina for their focus. Color posters—with the names of different colors written in another color, the word *green* written in purple, for example—can help develop impulse control. These activities require students to slow down—to pause—before acting, which strengthens their impulse control. Your class could play the "direction game," where you give each student a card with two directions on it, such as "Watch for someone to (clap hands, turn in a circle)" and "Then (say hello, stomp your feet)." Students must watch for a classmate to do the first direction on their card to know when they must do theirs. This activity helps students build stamina for remaining focused.

Building self-awareness is definitely a strategy that benefits from modeling. For example, when doing a read-aloud, stop to share your thinking about the book. As you share your thinking, model moving off topic, following a tangent, and then catching yourself and returning to your original focus. Have students talk about what they noticed you did. You may want to do this several times within a short period to help students identify what it looks like to notice when they move off topic and stop themselves.

For example, I model using Mo Willems's *Don't Let the Pigeon Stay Up Late* (2006). In the midst of the book, I stop to share what I am noticing about the text.

> I am noticing that the pigeon really doesn't want to go to bed. He is trying all kinds of strategies to not have to go to bed. He begs, he offers bribes, and he even threatens. He is really working hard. I love going to bed. It's one of my favorite times of day because I get

to read. Oh! I just got off topic. I was talking about the pigeon and what he was doing, and then I started thinking about how much I like going to bed. That does not really help me better understand this book.

If you have worked together to create a caring and supportive environment in your classroom, your students may respond to your modeling in generous ways. You will likely have children who speak up to support you and encourage you—and who may offer reasons why what you are doing is absolutely great. That can be tough when you're trying to model in this way, but it is definitely a positive thing for your class. You can thank them for their support and remind them that you make mistakes and that's OK. This is another example of modeling making mistakes, from Chapter 1, to help students feel more comfortable doing the same.

## Noticing a Move Off Topic

Sometimes it can be easier to notice that others are moving the conversation off topic. Students can get caught up in and excited about the various threads of their thinking and not be aware of when they move off track. If it is easier for your students to get started with this idea—noticing a move off topic—than it is to learn the self-management and self-awareness needed to stay on track, then this is a reasonable place to start. Noticing the track of a conversation as a listener rather than working on sharing their own thinking has a lower cognitive load. Noticing others straying off topic may also help students become more metacognitive about noticing their own tangents.

This strategy is easier for students to learn when they are highly invested in the discussion. They will be much more likely to try to hold the focus and fight against a move off topic if the topic is one they want to discuss. As mentioned earlier in this chapter, your students may find it easier to learn this strategy when the discussion surrounds a nonacademic topic (e.g., a popular TV show, video game, event in the community); this type of topic may be more interesting to them and also lowers the cognitive load. During the discussion, as students wander to a new topic, wait a bit to give other students a chance to refocus the conversation. If they don't do so, pause the conversation and ask the class if they feel they are still discussing the topic at hand. If they do refocus themselves, pause the conversation and highlight what happened. This noticing and naming when students are using or even approximating a skill will help you assess how well your students are mastering it. When you find yourself identifying strengths to notice and name more often and more quickly than you can keep up with, your students will definitely be ready to employ these skills in content-area conversations.

You can also try moving the cognitive load to the content sooner. If students are still struggling with tangents and straying off topic, you can return to nonacademic conversations. Raising and lowering the cognitive load can be fluid, as needed. At some points throughout the year, you may have to review some conversation skills and will need to lower the cognitive load on the content for a bit to give students a chance to firm up those skills.

**Responding to unprompted conversations.** During a morning meeting share in December, one of my students, Angie, shared about her "elf on a shelf." Our share time in the mornings isn't truly a conversation because students take turns sharing and calling on classmates for comments or questions. This particular morning, however, emotions surrounding the elf on a shelf were too much for that. One student responded to the share, "I don't want to offend anyone or anything and this is just my opinion, but I think the elf on a shelf is a bit creepy." Immediately other students jumped in to agree about the inherent creepiness or to argue in defense of the elf. This brief conversation offered me plenty to notice and name. I opted to focus on staying on topic. In this instance, I did not step in to refocus during the conversation. Eventually, a student asked Angie a question about where the elf was in her house. I waited for the end of the conversation and said,

> I noticed Angie started to talk about when she got her elf on a shelf. Then the conversation got off topic and people talked about whether or not the elf is creepy. Then Shannon got us back on topic by asking Angie a question about her elf. Sometimes we get so excited about our thinking, we forget to consider whether what we are sharing is really on topic for the conversation. It is helpful when someone else can help us get back on track.

With young children, noticing when a conversation has moved off topic is a skill that they can work on all year yet may still find challenging. Sometimes the work you're doing will feel frustrating and unhelpful. Remember, though, that even if students don't master identifying when they and their peers are moving off topic in conversations, they are building the foundation to do so. The practice and discussion will pay off, even if it is not until the next year and you aren't there to see it.

**Identifying productive tangents.** In addition, some tangents that take a conversation off topic can be quite beneficial, which adds to the complication of mastering this skill. You've likely seen this in your own conversations or in conversations in your classroom. The discussion is headed in one direction, someone poses a question or throws out an idea that makes for a serious U-turn or unexpected detour, and suddenly the conversation is opening up completely new avenues. So how do you—and then how do your students—know if a tangent is worth following or if the conversation needs to steer back in its original direction?

When I teach students to notice digressions and to bring the conversation back, I stick to that goal in redirecting and supporting their redirection of the talk—but if there's a tangent that seems promising, I make a note about it and bring it up for another conversation later.

Often when we have conversations about picture books, students make comments that are quite insightful, but not truly relevant to the current thread. I grab a sticky note and write down what I want to remember.

For example, in a discussion of *Who Says Women Can't Be Doctors? The Story of Elizabeth Blackwell* by Tanya Lee Stone (2013), the focus was on rules and laws that were unfair. One student said, "They've never seen a girl do it [be a doctor], so why do they think they can't?" I stuck a note with that question on my laptop, and we continued discussing unfair rules and laws. Later, I spent some time reflecting on how we could explore that question more deeply and think about our own biases based on what we haven't seen. It was a worthy question, but one that would have taken us off topic if we'd followed up on it right then. With young children, it's especially important not to muddy the waters when they're learning the difficult skill of keeping a conversation focused.

## Getting Back on Topic

The idea of getting back on topic is much less daunting than staying on topic or noticing a move off topic. If students are able to identify that a conversation is straying, bringing it back is not nearly as challenging. The part of this skill that can be difficult for young learners is holding on to the initial thread of the conversation. They must remember where the conversation was headed before it veered off track to return it to that course.

Modeling is a helpful strategy here, but you must be careful. When your students are having a conversation and you feel it is moving off topic, you will want to jump at the chance to model getting back on topic. That's the goal, right? Be prepared for your students to push back. This is a good thing for a couple of reasons. For one, if your students push back when you try to guide the conversation, you know they are deeply invested in it and that the class culture supports their beliefs in their own thinking and voices. That's powerful. The second reason that push-back is a good thing is that it is possible you were wrong. I have attempted to move a conversation back on topic only to have my students patiently explain to me how what they were saying was actually completely on topic. And usually they were right. Be open to the idea that what you thought was a tangent, really wasn't.

When you model, you're holding on to the thread of the conversation. Helping your students do the same is another step in the process. As described in Chapters 2 and 3, conversation mapping can help you see in what ways students are participating. Another strategy is developing a conversation summary; Figure 4.1 summarizes a class conversation about Kyle Lukoff's *When Aidan Became a Brother* (2019). Summarizing the conversation publicly and visibly for your students—on a whiteboard, chalkboard, or flip chart—can help them literally see which contributions are on topic. With really young students, documenting the conversation will have to be your task. With older students who are proficient writers, two or three of them could take notes on the conversation. This should probably not be done publicly unless the students truly feel up for it. Instead, keep it as a volunteer rather than an assigned task.

If you are able to keep a running record of the conversation in this way, when a student notices it heading off track, you can all look together at the record to see where the focus had previously been. In the conversation summarized in Figure 4.1, Daniela wondered why Aidan was worrying. Jefferson and Kimberly might have been connecting Aidan's worrying to their own moms' worrying, but they haven't made that clear; it appears they've moved the conversation off track. Keeping a visual record can be challenging because it requires quick summarizing of what students are saying as they continue to talk. It is worth doing, though, when you are sure you are ready to explicitly support students in getting back on topic.

FIGURE 4.1 | **SAMPLE CONVERSATION SUMMARY**

| Students | What they said | What I recorded |
| --- | --- | --- |
| Zhia | I think Aidan is really worried about being a good big brother to the new baby. | Aidan worried about being a good big brother. |
| Chris | I agree with Zhia. Aidan wants to do everything right. Everybody makes mistakes! | Aidan wants to do right. We make mistakes. |
| Daniela | Maybe Aidan is too worried. Why is he worrying so much? | Is Aidan worrying too much? |
| Jefferson | My mom worries a lot. She worries about everything. | J's mom worries. |
| Kimberly | My mom too! She is always worrying about me and my brother and my cousins and everything! | K's mom worries. |

Being able to find the language to return the focus in a conversation may challenge students. Many children don't want to feel they are accusing their peers of being wrong. (Of course, other young children don't have any problem with that.) Sentence starters can help those who are hesitant to redirect a conversation because they don't want to upset a classmate to find the right words. Such sentence starters can be as simple as "We were talking about . . . ." Other sentence starters that might help are actually questions, such as "Can you help me understand how this is related to _____ that we were discussing?" I use questions a lot with my students. Doing so signifies my belief in them and their ideas and suggests that I'm not understanding the connection rather than that the connection doesn't exist.

Noticing when a conversation is straying and moving to return it to the main focus is a bit like making a wrong turn on a journey. If you're lucky, your GPS will immediately recalculate and offer you a way to keep moving forward. If not, you may struggle a bit to work your way back to the original path to keep heading to your destination. At first, your students' conversations may feel a lot like getting off course with no GPS. As long as they're working toward that original path, allow students to struggle a bit. If they're feeling frustrated or unable to get back to the topic, step in and support—but don't jump in too soon. Don't underestimate your students' abilities to find their way together. Over time, they'll hone these skills and collaborate to function more like the GPS in getting quickly back on track.

> **Sentence Starters: Staying on and Getting Back on Topic**
>
> I think we're getting off topic.
>
> I'm not sure if we're still talking about the question at hand.
>
> We were talking about....
>
> Can we get back to discussing....?

## Assessing Staying and Getting Back on Topic

The skills discussed in this chapter rely a lot on metacognition: They require students to be aware of their own thoughts, both those that are on track and those that are distractions. Self-assessment can be useful for all of the skills in this chapter, both for your understanding of students' progress and as students push to even deeper awareness of their use of these skills. Self-assessments can be informal or formal, depending on your goals. Because students are just beginning to build their stamina for staying on topic, you may want to start with more informal but frequent self-assessments.

Informal self-assessment can be as simple as pausing a conversation and having students reflect on their focus with a "fist of five."

Ask students, "How well is your brain focused on the topic of our conversation?" They then hold up fingers, from zero to five. Zero means they are not on topic at all, and five indicates a complete focus on the topic at hand. Because a fist of five offers a wide range of responses, you might find it more useful to ask students to rate themselves on a scale of one to three instead. The idea is to pause students and force their reflection on how well they have been focused on the topic of the discussion.

For a more formal, but similar, way to self-assess focusing skills, use a written reflection activity following the end of a conversation. Your students should rank how well they were focused on the topic during the conversation, but then add an explanation. It may help them if you provide prompts for more information, such as, "I got off topic (in my head or in my talk) when . . . ," and "I refocused my attention on the topic by . . . ." Using both prompts can be helpful in promoting student self-reflection. The first prompt assumes that all students get off topic at some point. This may not be true, but it normalizes it happening and makes it OK for students to admit to it. The second prompt helps students notice what they, personally, do to get back on track so that they can do it again in the future. Having students share their responses to the second prompt can help others as well. Hearing strategies their friends use to refocus on the topic offers students ideas to try if they feel at a loss.

## Connecting Ideas

Connecting ideas is where all of the previous work comes together in having conversations help build new understandings. When students are able to take ideas from others and connect them, they are building something new in their own learning. This can happen in a couple of different ways. Students can connect their own thinking to ideas or questions they hear shared by a peer. **Connecting one's own idea** to another's builds on the ideas from Chapter 3 surrounding agreeing and disagreeing and adding on to others' ideas. Students might also **connect the ideas of others.** In this instance, it isn't their own thinking they are bringing together; it is the ideas or questions from two or more of their peers. This skill requires advanced listening and processing skills.

## Connecting One's Own Idea to Another's

You know that look on students' faces when they make a connection? The one that lets you practically see the lightbulb going on over their heads? That's the result of connections being made. When students are able to bring ideas together, they have that "aha!" moment.

I live in a large, crowded, suburban area. For reasons that escape me, many of the streets in our area change names. As my oldest daughter has been learning to drive, she's finally learning street names. When she realizes, for example, that Hillside Road and Forrester Road are the same road, just on opposite sides of Rolling Road, she gets that look on her face. She's made that connection between the two—really one—roads. The goal is for students, through their conversations, to be connecting the different ideas they are thinking and hearing in this same way. Being able to do so will allow them to move forward on their journey of learning.

Just as with the skills of staying on topic and getting back on topic, connecting ideas is difficult to see. Because it is something that is happening inside a person's head, bringing that out into the light can be a challenge. By the time you are ready to explicitly teach this skill, it is likely that some of your students have already used it in classroom conversations. So when you are ready to begin specifically addressing this skill, you can notice and name when students are using it. "I noticed that Oscar heard an idea from Luci and connected it to what he was thinking. He put his idea and Luci's idea together to help him understand more." Again, noticing and naming not only helps students identify and gain language for a conversational skill, but also validates what they are already doing and encourages them to continue doing it.

This skill is another one that definitely benefits from modeling. During an interactive read-aloud or when students explain their thinking about a science experiment, you can model connecting ideas, to concretely show how this skill sounds. You might say,

> I just heard Fatima say that our ladybug larvae don't look like ladybugs yet. I was remembering the caterpillars from 2nd grade and how they made chrysalises to become butterflies. Now I'm thinking that our ladybug larvae are going to do the same thing. Fatima's observation and my thinking about the butterflies helped me come up with a new idea about our ladybugs.

Unlike the skills discussed in previous chapters, teaching students to connect ideas requires more planning and thought to model well. I can typically model adding *because* or asking questions on the fly during a lesson. Connecting ideas requires me to think ahead. When I think my students are ready for this skill, I'll take some time before lessons to think about the kinds of ideas or questions they might share and how I could connect with them. If I don't plan and think this through ahead of time, I might find myself modeling the skill without noticing and not highlighting it for my students, completely missing the opportunity to connect. On the plus side, doing the thoughtful planning ahead for modeling connecting ideas makes this easier to do and comes more naturally over time.

For direct teaching of this skill, pause the conversation, and ask students to think about what they have heard others share and then to think about how one of those ideas or questions connects to something they were thinking. You might ask older students to write down ideas, and younger children to talk with a partner about their ideas. At first this can feel a bit forced. Many students will feel uncomfortable with it and will not be able to—or won't feel they are able to—connect to anyone else's ideas. This is OK, and they need to know it's OK. The goal is to get them to stop, think about what they are hearing, and think about their own ideas. Some students will definitely want to share. Their connections may be loose or rough, and that's also OK. Approximations of the skill are a great start.

These more metacognitive skills addressed in this chapter are supported by noticing and naming. Carefully watch your students and celebrate when they try these new skills. Being supportive of their attempts encourages students and motivates them to keep trying.

## Connect the Ideas of Others

As challenging as it can be to bring together one's own thinking with others', connecting the ideas of others raises the difficulty level even more. Students will need to be deeply listening and considering what they're hearing to realize that Hillside Road and Forester Road are actually connected. Reminding them of the listening skills they have practiced and used is an important step in this process.

That said, many of the metacognitive skills for connecting one's own ideas will help support connecting the ideas of others. You will need to model this for your students, just as you modeled connecting your thinking. Bringing together two or more threads in a conversation and explicitly sharing that with your students gives them a framework to try. "Wow, Jared noticed the character seems worried and Stephanie talked about how her friend seems to be ignoring her. I'm thinking she's worrying about her friendship and why her friend might be mad at her." Jared and Stephanie may both have been thinking exactly that, but not explaining it thoroughly. Your modeling will help your students make their thinking more concrete and able to be seen by themselves and others.

Because this skill is not as easily visible as others, it can be helpful to pause the conversation for some specific thinking or writing time. Allow a conversation to flow, giving several students a chance to share their thinking or ask questions. Then, pause the conversation and have students write down or think about what they've heard their classmates saying. Ask them if they're noticing any connections between those ideas and questions. Some students will likely not identify any connections at first, and others may identify connections that seem weak or even nonexistent. That's still a good start! Have you ever noticed how young children, upon learning how to use an exclamation mark or comma, will insert these everywhere? Sometimes a young child's writing will have an exclamation mark after every word. That's a sign that the student is trying out this new learning, approximating what should be done. You'll see the same behavior as they learn the skill of connecting ideas: students will make attempts or feel at a loss, and it will take some time to help them see when the exclamation mark really fits. Again, identify and celebrate their attempts. Building up their confidence as thinkers encourages them to continue trying and sharing what they're thinking.

> **Sentence Starters: Connecting Ideas**
>
> It sounds like what _____ is saying is connected to my thinking because . . . .
>
> I noticed when _____ said _____, it made me think about when _____ said _____, because . . . .
>
> That idea goes with what _____ said because . . . .

## Assessing Connecting Ideas

I have not yet discussed rubrics, a common assessment tool. One reason for this omission is that these skills look very different for kindergartners than they might for 3rd graders or for 5th graders. Rubrics are an option if they are designed to specifically meet the needs of your students. Connecting ideas comprises a set of complex skills; using a rubric can help you assess whether your students are mastering this strategy (see Figure 4.2 for an example).

FIGURE 4.2 | **RUBRIC FOR ASSESSING CONNECTING IDEAS**

| Skills | 1 | 2 | 3 | 4 |
|---|---|---|---|---|
| Connecting your own ideas to others' | Student does not connect their own ideas to others. | Student states a connection without explanation. | Student names a connection and gives a basic explanation. | Student names a connection and explains deeply. |
| Connecting the ideas of others | Student does not connect the ideas of others. | Student states that others' ideas are connected without explanation. | Student names a connection between others' ideas and gives a basic explanation. | Student names a connection between others' ideas and explains deeply. |

A simple checklist to note whether students are making connections (such as that used when assessing listening skills; see Chapter 3) will give you some basic information, but it will not show you how meaningful students' connections are. A rubric gets at that level of detail. Some of your students will not connect ideas at all. Others will say things like "I have a connection with Allison" with no explanation for that connection. You will also have students who say, "I have a connection with Allison because I was also thinking the character was scared when that happened," making clear the nature of this connection. Finally, you will have students who say things like, "I have a connection with Allison because I was thinking the character was scared too. He was having trouble speaking and he was thinking of running away. That made me think he was scared." Such students are making the connection, naming it, and developing their own thinking through it.

You can adapt the Figure 4.2 rubric with a space to list students' names below each column. As students make connections, write their name in the column that best fits the thoughts they shared. This will mean that some students will have their name in more than one column if they make multiple connections. At the end of the conversation, review this detailed rubric. Who is taking on these skills? Who isn't? Across the class, how strongly are these skills developing? If many of your students are at 3 or 4, you are making solid progress. If not, then you will be able to see where your students need more practice with these skills.

## Including Others

In any conversation, some individuals speak frequently and others do so rarely or not at all. If you have ever participated in a book club, you can probably easily picture those who spoke frequently, but those who rarely spoke may not come to mind as quickly. Children should be explicitly taught about silences and purposeful pauses in conversations; both students inclined to speak and those disinclined will have to work at including everyone in conversations. Students who do not speak frequently or do not speak at all in conversations may be holding back for a variety of reasons; consider what might be keeping a child from participating before taking action to encourage them to do so. Some students lack confidence about sharing their ideas at all or lack the confidence to speak up in the brief silences between others. Others require more time to think than is possible during a fast-paced conversation. Still others may be disengaged and not truly listening to the conversation, so they are unable to participate. Students' facial expressions and body language can provide some clues about the reasons they are quiet.

Students who have a lot to say and the confidence to say it, on the other hand, can find it challenging to include others. Students who speak often and have a tendency to dominate the conversation need to learn to share the space. One of the first things students must learn and be willing to do is to sit with the silence. Teaching students to **pause and breathe** will push them to stop and give space for other voices. Teaching students to **read people** will be helpful in building their ability to **invite others into a conversation** respectfully and gently.

## Pause and Breathe

Young students who have a lot to share, and the confidence to share it, often have difficulty allowing for silences. Their excitement about sharing makes it challenging for them to wait for an opportunity to speak. Your goal is to encourage those students to continue sharing their thinking while also helping them learn to give others the space to share as well. One way to work toward this is to teach students to pause and breathe. When a student finishes speaking, everyone else should take three slow, deep breaths. Doing this forces a silence in the space. It gives quieter students or those who need a bit more processing time a chance to prepare to speak.

This strategy isn't perfect. Students who cannot wait to speak will make their breaths quicker to get their voices in before anyone else does. It will take some time and practice before your most eager students are able to use their impulse control here; you might need to revisit self-management skills (see Chapter 1) and explore strategies to help students develop and increase their impulse control.

One example is the Bell Game. Give each student a small bell and have them walk around the room. The goal is to not make any sound from the bell. You can make the walk more complicated by putting obstacles in the way. You can also do this at recess to add new challenges. Direction Lag and Simon Says Do the Opposite are two more. In Direction Lag, the leader gives the class a direction, and they wait for the next one. When the leader gives the second direction, the class follows the first one. They continue following directions, always one direction behind. This requires them to control the impulse to do the direction being given at the time. Simon Says Do the Opposite is similar. If Simon says stand, students should sit. If Simon says stomp your right foot, students should stomp their left foot. All of these games require students to control the impulse to act on the initial urge. Keep reminding students to pause and breathe, and celebrate when they clearly make the attempt to wait and give that space and silence to their classmates.

You can exert more control in this area in other ways, if you feel it is necessary. You can have students share in smaller, homogeneous groups: students who speak frequently can be in one group and those who tend not to speak can be in another. This grouping will give quieter students some wait time and can build their confidence to share in a larger group setting. Another possibility is to give each student three blocks (or stickers or tiles). Each time a student speaks during a conversation, they put down one of their blocks. When all of their blocks are on the ground, they are finished speaking for that conversation. This approach will help you limit some students from dominating the conversation.

Another possibility is to arrange students for the conversation in an inner circle and an outer circle, with students who do not typically speak in whole-class conversations composing the inner circle. For the first part of the discussion, only those in the inner circle speak. Similar to the strategy of homogeneous small groups for conversations, this gives students the wait time and space to speak up. This setting also allows your more talkative students to hear from their quieter classmates. After a while, the two circles can merge and continue the conversation, allowing the chattier students to add to and build on their classmates' ideas. This activity will help your chattier students see the value in what their peers have to say and help them encourage participation from others more often.

You should not need to use these strategies indefinitely, bearing in mind that the ultimate goal is for your students to be productive, respectful conversationalists independently, without support from you. As with the other content you are teaching, however, use the supports and strategies needed to help your students grow. As they need those supports and strategies less and less, you can remove the scaffolding.

## Reading People

Students who speak often and are learning to allow silences may be ready to explore how to invite others into a conversation. Doing so requires an awareness of their own participation as well as the participation of other members in the group, which is a lot for young students to consider. It is tricky for another reason as well: inviting another into a conversation must be done in a genuine way. Students must truly value one another's ideas and thinking for their peers to feel the invitation is meaningful. Students also must be able to invite in a kind way, rather than in a way that makes others feel uncomfortable or put on the spot. Everyone in the class needs to know that their voice is valued and, at the same time, that they are not required to share during any given conversation.

Therefore, one of the skills students may need to learn to be able to invite others in with kindness and genuineness is to read people—to read facial expressions and body language. Students should be learning to identify when their classmates might have something to say and when they are anxious or uncomfortable. Role-playing activities can help students with this. A teacher or student can model interest in speaking (leaning forward, mouth open, eyes watching the group) and students can name what they are seeing that shows this interest. Modeling anxiety about speaking (e.g., closed-off body language, eyes looking down, tense facial muscles), on the other hand, needs to be done carefully so as not to make any student feel singled out.

Watching conversations from movies and TV also can help your students notice body language and facial expressions, especially if you do so without any sound. Animated shows are not great for this, but episodes of *Sesame Street* or other live-action shows offer opportunities for your students to read people without having to worry about upsetting someone, which might happen if they practice this skill with their peers. Play just a short clip with clear body language and facial expressions for your class. Ask them how they think one of the characters is feeling and why they think that.

Another way for students to increase their skill at reading others is to have them practice acting like they feel a certain way—sort of like charades, but with emotions. Students can pantomime an emotion. Start simple, with "happy" and "mad." Have them show they are feeling that way and then notice and name what their face looks like and what they are doing with their body. They can look around at one another as well, to notice how their classmates present these emotions. Then you can move to more complicated emotions, such as "worry," "eagerness," or "frustration." Being able to read people is a skill that will serve your students in many different settings and ways: in friendships, with authority figures, and in social situations, for example.

### Invite Others into a Conversation

The final step in students really learning together is for them to be able to invite others into a conversation. When students do this, they are showing that they value the ideas and perspectives of others and that they value the opportunity to learn from others. To be able to invite others, students need to be able to give others the space and silence to speak if they want to do so. They must notice who is still not speaking. Finally, they should invite respectfully, noting the facial expressions and body language of the others in the conversation.

It can be helpful to think of this as a multistep process, for both your students and you. The first couple of steps include the strategies of pausing to breathe and reading people. As students are working on those skills, you can begin modeling inviting others in. This will help students when they are ready to try it, while also strengthening the community in your classroom and valuing of all voices.

When students demonstrate that they are waiting patiently and giving others a chance to share, you can make your modeling more explicit. When you invite a student into the conversation, you might say, "Julia, would you like to add anything to the conversation?" After Julia responds and shares (or declines to share), you can say,

> I noticed Julia had not said anything in our conversation. I saw that she had been listening carefully, and her facial expression showed me that she was really thinking about what we have been discussing. I was really curious to hear what she was thinking if she wanted to share it.

Using this precise language does several things. Saying "I noticed Julia had not said anything in our conversation" shows students that you are paying attention to who is and is not speaking. They will learn that they can do the same thing. "I saw that she had been listening carefully, and her facial expression showed me that she was really thinking about what we have been discussing" lets students know that there was a reason you asked Julia to share. You didn't randomly choose a student who hadn't spoken up; you asked someone whose body language and facial expressions showed investment in the conversation. Finally, "I was really curious to hear what she was thinking if she wanted to share it" models two things: (1) it shows students that you value their thinking and that you want to hear what they will share, and (2) it reminds students that they are in charge of their learning; they get to decide if they want to share or not.

Inviting others in can be emotional not just for the inviter, but especially for the invitee. You may want to check in with students after a conversation to gauge how they felt about having been invited (or having invited someone). Many young students will be fine with having been invited or even feel special because of it. You definitely need to be aware, however, of those who are uncomfortable, to assess their feelings and determine how to respond. Some students just need to be reassured that being invited is actually a choice and not a requirement and learn that it's OK to say no. Other students may need to hear that being invited is a sign of how much their classmates value their thinking. Still others may not be ready to share in whole-group conversations and just need to practice saying, "No thanks," when they are invited in.

It is amazing to watch young children engage in a conversation when they are taking on all of these skills: listening to one another, sharing thinking, and including others in the conversation. This does not happen overnight, but over time you will see your students using these skills independently, outside your classroom conversations.

## Assessing Including Others

Unlike evaluating whether students' comments are on topic and how well they are connecting ideas, it will be clear when students invite others in. The other strategies I've discussed in this chapter, pausing to breathe and reading people, have a specific purpose (i.e., to give others a chance to speak), but I don't always assess them for every student. Students who dominate conversations and speak frequently—usually about a quarter to a third of my class—are the ones who need to practice these skills the most. As a result, on occasion I

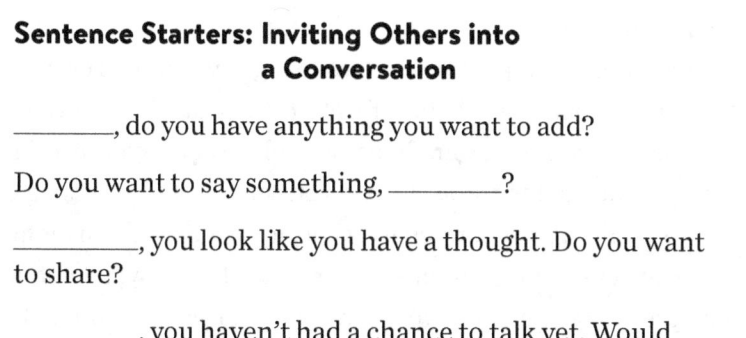

**Sentence Starters: Inviting Others into a Conversation**

_____, do you have anything you want to add?

Do you want to say something, _____?

_____, you look like you have a thought. Do you want to share?

_____, you haven't had a chance to talk yet. Would you like to?

will set up a checklist with just those students' names and watch them throughout a conversation to see if they are taking time to pause and breathe and if they are watching their classmates to read people.

One final note on assessing conversation skills in general: Think about the myriad ways you assess your students' knowledge and skills on a daily (even hourly) basis. The longer you've been teaching, the more fluent and fluid your assessing likely is. You've gained knowledge over time about what it looks like when students are developing their knowledge and skills. Knowing what it looks like when a student uses a conversation skill well is foundational to being able to assess them. Reflect on how you want students to use these skills. As an adult who engages in all kinds of conversations, you are probably using these conversation skills regularly. Your students are not as proficient as you yet, but knowing how the skills look when *you* use them will help you gauge your students' progress. The more your students practice their conversation skills, the clearer it will be where they can go with them. It won't take long to have a good sense of what your kindergartners or 2nd graders can do with sharing their own thinking, and this will help you assess in the future.

As a classroom teacher who is assessing anything and everything all the time, I am a firm believer in finding strategies and routines that make assessing as simple as possible. You may already have forms or routines for assessing that you can adapt to assessing conversation skills. The seating chart recording has been a win for me. It was a way of assessing that made sense quickly and, while not being super-easy to take on, felt worth the work for what I gained. I also rely frequently on checklists and self-assessments. What matters is capturing the talk moves your students are making in a way that will be accessible to you and allow you to plan for the future.

---

One of the most noticeable results of students synthesizing thinking will be when they change their minds. This won't (and shouldn't) always happen; students can synthesize thinking without changing their minds. When you see students revise their thinking, however, you are seeing the results of their taking on others' ideas and connecting these to their own thoughts. Changing one's mind requires vulnerability and a willingness to accept that one might have been wrong. For students to be able to demonstrate this, they need to be in a culture of acceptance and risk taking. Without that culture, it is far less likely children will be ready and willing to change their minds.

So much of schooling is about getting the "right" answer. Children learn from a young age that having the right answer is valued and rewarded. Teachers have to actively work to help children see that getting the correct answer is not always the ultimate goal because a laser focus on the right answer can, at times, hinder actual learning. It can keep students from seeing broader perspectives, and it can hold students back from taking risks and stretching themselves as learners. In addition, sometimes getting to the correct answer is not a straight shot and involves revising one's thinking. And—even more radical for some students to consider—in some situations there may not be a right answer.

The ultimate goal in academic conversations is deeper understanding and ongoing learning. Finding the "right" answer usually results in an ending, with students stopping their learning at that point. This may be fine at times, but building the skills to continue learning outside and beyond school requires more than simply getting to one specific answer. These conversation skills will have students sharing their thinking, exploring others' thinking, and bringing it all together to build new ideas and new questions. They can use these skills for the rest of their lives to continue learning and to be active, valuable citizens.

# 5

# NAVIGATING DISAGREEMENTS

As your students engage in conversations with others that encourage them to share their ideas, explore others' ideas, and bring all of that thinking together, they will likely run into some disagreements. No matter how well individuals explain their thinking and listen to others, there will still be times when they do not come to a consensus. This can present a few challenges for you.

In academic conversations—as in many other types of conversations—there will be things that are factual and true. If your students are in disagreement about facts, you will probably feel a need to correct that. I'm going to suggest that you should not immediately do so. You can feel the need, but you should fight against it. Carol Garhart Mooney (2000) related a story of young students arguing about who could and could not be nurses and doctors. At the end of their disagreement,

> the teacher quietly concluded [that] it sounded as though they all knew different things about doctors and nurses, but that it was

true that men and women worked at both jobs. By letting the children continue their arguments and discussions, she nurtured not only the content of the conversation but also the process which will help them all become better learners. (pp. 90–91)

Academic conversations help students become more independent in their learning and that is an important goal. If you always step in quickly to correct them, students will continue to rely on you to do so. As Lucy West and Antonia Cameron noted (2013),

> For students to share their ideas with their teacher and classmates on how something works, why a war was fought and whether war is ever moral, how to solve a mystifying mathematics problem, or argue for the merits of a particular character in the historical novel, then teachers have to refrain from doing these things for students and invite students to share their ideas and to think critically about the ideas and opinions of others. (p. 2)

Allowing students to disagree, even when it means someone is wrong, is an important part of this learning process. It can be helpful to think of the differences between *argumentation* and *arguing*. Argumentation requires students to engage with evidence, make their claims, and identify areas in which they disagree. "They can disagree without being disagreeable, and they can interact in sophisticated ways as they solve problems" (Smith, Fisher, & Frey, 2015, p. 38).

Another challenge that arises when students are not coming to consensus in a conversation can be their emotional responses. Many young children have a strong sense of being "right" in their thinking and ideas. When others disagree, it can evoke powerful feelings. Again, this is true for adults in many conversations as well. I am sure you can think of a conversation with a spouse or sibling that got heated, even though it was about something that seemed silly later. For me, it is often conversations about who has or has not cleaned certain kitchen items more frequently. My husband and I both get up in arms when such topics come up in our house. Ann R. Eisenberg, (1987), writing about the ways children argue with others noted that "arguments may often lead to aggressive or disruptive behavior" (p. 114), but students can practice certain strategies and language to make that less common. As your students learn to say, "I disagree with _____ *because* . . . ," they are gaining the skills needed. "Children seem eager to use the word *disagree* to be able to express their opposition to another person's ideas in an acceptable and polite manner" (Clark et al., 2003, p. 192). Disagreement doesn't always bring strong emotions, but it quite easily can, and it is something you need to help students learn to navigate.

It's important to note that the goal is not to make sure all students agree by the end of a conversation. My husband and I are highly unlikely to ever agree about who does more of certain kitchen work. The goal is to help students grow the skills to disagree in conversations in ways that are healthy and productive, rather than in ways that set up roadblocks to learning and can damage relationships. Lacking the skills to disagree with respect and thoughtfulness can be dangerous. Think of all the models—on television news and other shows or in movies—of disagreements that are verbally combative and more about "winning" the conversation than about productive learning or sharing of ideas.

Certain social-emotional skills are foundational to being able to engage in conversations productively and meaningfully. In this chapter, we will take a look at specific skills that help students navigate disagreements, **competencies identified by the Collaborative for Academic, Social, and Emotional Learning** (CASEL), which are essential to seeing other perspectives. We will also **review the foundational skills** discussed in the preceding chapters with an eye toward how those skills can support students in challenging conversations and look at some strategies for helping students **understand another's perspective.** The skills addressed in this chapter are closely linked to skills in, or are repeated from, earlier chapters. The focus here is on students' social-emotional skills in conversations because **navigating disagreements** can be more emotionally challenging than previous strategies. When supporting students through disagreements, you can use the assessment strategies noted in earlier chapters.

## Social-Emotional Competencies

The five CASEL (2020) competencies have been a part of all the work in previous chapters, but they are especially important in helping students to navigate disagreements. The CASEL competencies articulate "what students should know and be able to do for academic success, school and civic engagement, health and wellness, and fulfilling careers" (p. 2). The goals of academic conversations align with these items, especially academic success and school and civic engagement, requiring a deeper exploration of the competencies.

### Self-Awareness

Although the five competencies are tightly woven together and students' development in these skills is not sequential, **self-awareness** does have a foundational feel. CASEL (2020) defines the competency of self-awareness as comprising "abilities to understand one's own emotions, thoughts, and values and how they influence behavior across contexts" (p. 2). For young learners, identifying their own emotions is a necessary first step toward interacting with others in positive ways. Even as an adult, I struggle at times with self-awareness. I can recognize that I feel out of sorts or not myself but am unable to identify why. Understanding what is happening emotionally is more challenging for young children, of course, because they have less experience doing so.

To navigate disagreements, students must have some self-awareness to identify how they are feeling. As I've noted, disagreements can raise strong emotions, and if students are unaware of those emotions and how they are affecting their behavior, they are likely to respond in unproductive ways. Again, think of times you or someone close to you has responded in a way that feels outsized for the topic, when a small request or seemingly innocuous statement was met with anger or anxiety or depression. Adults are often able to take a step back (as either the initiator or the responder) in such a scenario and identify why that response occurred. Maybe the request or topic is one that triggers some trauma, or maybe the responder was having a difficult time, unrelated to that conversation, and those difficulties spilled out. Whatever it is, being able to identify the cause and the emotions allows adults to make a productive change.

This is true for children as well. Students need the tools and the space to build self-awareness. One way to help them do this is to pause the conversation when disagreements arise during academic conversations (and before anyone gets strongly emotional). Say to students, "It sounds like Diego and Elise disagree about this. How is that making you feel?" Ask the question of all students, but definitely make sure to look at or somehow subtly check in with Diego and Elise. Posing the question to everyone allows the students in the heat of a disagreement to take a moment and focus on their emotions and helps them build a habit of doing so.

You can also model your own reflection:

> I'm noticing Diego and Elise are disagreeing about this. When people disagree, I sometimes get worried. I want people to get along. Diego and Elise are talking about their disagreement, and they are not fighting, but I noticed I'm still feeling a little bit worried. Is anyone noticing how they are feeling right now?

Modeling your own reflection not only gives students some language they can use and a clear example of self-awareness, but also makes this practice explicit. You do not need to say you are helping students become more self-aware, but you do want to be sure students know that you are helping them identify their emotions. Don't assume students will understand the purposes behind the moves you are making; spell it out for them. Pausing conversations before emotions rise gives students some time and space to practice self-awareness, while also setting them up for self-management.

## Self-Management

The competency of self-management is closely related to self-awareness: both involve intrapersonal skills. Pausing a conversation when a disagreement arises gives students the opportunity to identify their emotions. They then also have the opportunity to make a more conscious decision about how to proceed, in light of those emotions. This is a wonderful time to bring back *Hunter and His Amazing Remote Control* (Copeland, 1998; see Chapter 1). Remind students that they know how to hit their "remote control" to pause, relax, and think about how they want to proceed.

This modeling can also demonstrate self-awareness. After explaining to students how you are feeling worried because of the disagreement, you can share thoughts on how you respond to those feelings.

> When I feel worried like this, I want to stop the disagreement. I might tell Diego and Elise that they're both right and it is just fine. But I know that won't help us learn together here, and because Diego and Elise are talking and not fighting about this, I don't think they need my help. I really have to pause to think about that though. My immediate reaction is to jump in and try to make things better. I think what I really need to do, instead, is to listen more.

Supporting students in their development of self-awareness and self-management is challenging because these competencies are not always easy to see. Because these are intrapersonal skills, the work is all happening internally. It may be obvious to you that a student is making progress compared to what they have previously demonstrated, but it will be difficult to help young children recognize it as clearly. Because these skills are personal and intimate, you may want to notice and name more privately when students are doing them well. After a whole-group conversation, pull a student aside to share with them how you noticed their self-management skills. You might say,

> I noticed you were leaning forward, bouncing a bit, and rubbing your hands together when Diego and Elise were disagreeing. You must have had a lot you wanted to say, but you waited and listened to them instead. That must have been hard, but you did it.

Identifying for students something they did well makes it more likely they will want to do it again; it also helps them clearly see their successes. Sometimes they do things well and don't actually realize it. Students need to know when they are successful, especially with something that has been challenging for them.

## Social Awareness

Social awareness, according to the CASEL (2020) description, includes "abilities to understand the perspectives of and empathize with others, including those from diverse backgrounds, cultures, and contexts" (p. 2). The examples for this competency seem perfectly designed for navigating disagreements:

- Recognizing strengths in others
- Demonstrating empathy and compassion
- Showing concern for the feelings of others
- Taking others' perspectives

Taking, or seeing, others' perspectives is something we will be exploring in depth later in this chapter. It is a difficult thing for many people to do, but it is essential for participation in conversations that have the potential for becoming emotional. The other examples are directly related to the community of a classroom and group of students. If you have all worked together to create a culture of support and risk taking, students will be much closer to recognizing the strengths of their classmates as well as to showing empathy, compassion, and concern for others' feelings.

This is also an area in which literature can play a role. You can support social awareness by reading picture books and practicing these skills toward the characters. It is often easier to do this with fictional characters than it is with real people. Fictional characters have not hurt our feelings or annoyed us in the way that our peers do on a regular basis.

When you are noticing and naming students using various skills, you are recognizing their strengths. This does not have to fall to you alone. Your students can also notice and name when they see their peers use skills they are practicing. In my 3rd grade classroom, we have a board with sentence starters and skills, with sticky notes nearby. At first, I grab a few sticky notes after a conversation, tell students what I observed, and write it down to post on the board. With a little encouragement (and sometimes even without any prompting from me), my students begin writing notes themselves. They recognize the strengths of others.

Showing concern for the feelings of others and demonstrating empathy and compassion are closely related and often look quite similar. Students are developing these skills quite clearly when they are working on including others, especially reading people and inviting others in (see Chapter 4). Understanding others' facial expressions and body language to determine if someone wants to be a part of the conversation or if that would make them uncomfortable and acting on that knowledge are a part of showing concern for the feelings of others.

At Thanksgiving, in many schools, young students dress up as Native Americans and Pilgrims as a part of their learning in class. One year my 1st grade students had quite the conversation about this tradition. Although there was strong disagreement about whether this was an acceptable practice, students on both sides of the discussion demonstrated empathy and compassion, for their classmates and for others. Those arguing for the tradition suggested that kindergartners are "just little kids and the teachers want them to have fun." Those students demonstrated empathy and compassion for the kindergartners, thinking about the joy they would feel participating in this tradition. Students on the other side argued that "it's disrespectful; they don't even get the costumes right," showing empathy for Native Americans who are misrepresented this way. Although many students felt strongly about the topic, their social-emotional skills were strong enough to support their engagement in a disagreement without anger or unkindness. Their social awareness skills were crucial to that conversation.

## Relationship Skills

This competency, according to CASEL (2020), is about forming "healthy and supportive relationships" (p. 2) and continuing them over time. Although many adults may be most likely to disagree with those closest to them (as much because they talk with those people more than anyone else), they are also able to navigate those disagreements more easily because of the strong relationship. Having established relationships can help one navigate disagreements more successfully. You care for the other person or people involved and don't want to hurt them, even when you disagree. Young children have a pretty good understanding of this, which can be seen when they talk with family and close friends. Disagreements rarely—not never but rarely—get out of control and affect the relationship beyond that moment. Your task, then, is to help your students navigate disagreements with classmates and others with whom they do not have such strong prior relationships just as productively. The skills discussed in previous chapters and the social-emotional learning skills will play a role in this. Relationship skills are strongly affected by the work you've done and continue doing to foster a community and build a sense of trust in your classroom.

## Responsible Decision Making

Responsible decision making is as much about a person's individual behavior and choices as it is about social interactions. One of the CASEL (2020) examples for this competency is "anticipating and evaluating the consequences of one's actions" (p. 2). Anticipation can be difficult for young children. They don't have the wealth of life experience to turn to as they look forward. "When we undergo an experience, our brain cells—called neurons—become active" (Siegel & Bryson, 2011, p. 7). It is difficult to anticipate consequences if you have not seen the situation before or have not seen it often. Imagine traveling to another country where words, phrases, facial expressions, and hand gestures mean something different than what you've always known. It will be challenging to anticipate the consequences of saying a certain phrase or gesturing in a certain way if the consequences are not what you've seen again and again.

Young students are often shocked by the effects of their words or actions. Either they could not empathize with another's perspective, or they were unable to anticipate what might happen—or, honestly, both can be true.

# Revisiting Skills

In the preceding chapters, we explored ways students can share their own thinking, understand the thinking of others, and synthesize and bring it all together. The skills they have been using to do all of those things will be useful in navigating disagreements. If students have been developing those skills and using them independently in academic conversations, they will have a strong foundation for engaging in conversations that are more challenging or more emotional. Doing so requires the ability to share their side of the disagreement and also to listen and (at least try to) understand what others are saying.

Just as you shouldn't expect students to immediately demonstrate and use all of these skills in an academic conversation, you can't expect them to immediately generalize these during significant disagreements. If a disagreement is getting emotional between students, you will have to decide which strategies and skills will be most useful in helping them navigate the current disagreement. You can remind them of those skills or model them in the moment, but you will have to make decisions about what will be the most powerful. The first step is to notice what students are doing well in the disagreement to determine where they might need more support. Many of the strategies suggested in this chapter involve pausing students during a disagreement. That pause will help them regroup and use their skills—and it also gives you a moment to reflect on what you are noticing and make an instructional decision about how to move forward.

## Skills for Sharing One's Thinking

It can become harder to share one's own thinking when faced with disagreement. Emotional investment in the conversation takes over and makes it difficult to be as thoughtful as one might usually be. Reinforcing the skills from this chapter will help students keep the focus on the ideas and organize their thinking. **Supporting and clarifying skills** are essential to navigating disagreements.

In disagreements, when emotions take over, students often lose sight of the supports for their ideas. Reminding students to add *because* to what they are saying (see Chapter 2) will help them make a stronger argument. Elaborating or rephrasing can help listeners better understand. Clarifying what one is saying frequently resolves a disagreement because the listener wasn't clear about what was being said or they misunderstood the thinking process. The goal is not always to make the disagreement go away. Plenty of disagreements will remain no matter how thoughtful a conversation might be or how long it could go on. Students need to learn to accept that and to navigate such situations. For disagreements that result from a misunderstanding, however, students being able to support their thinking and clarify what they are saying can make a significant difference. Supporting and clarifying will focus any conversation and help listeners, both those engaging in the conversation and those who are only listening, learn and grow together.

## Skills for Understanding the Thinking of Others

As discussed in Chapter 4, conversations are two-way streets. One hopes that all participants in a conversation will use the skills for sharing one's thinking. Listeners must flip their role and work to understand the thinking of those speaking, as they support and clarify.

One of the things that often does *not* happen in disagreements is the most basic of these skills: listening. Because emotions can be high in disagreements, the participants are thinking so much about their own ideas and perspectives that they don't listen to others. Or they don't truly listen and actually hear what is being said. True, meaningful listening requires active participation and mental effort. As Dominique Smith, Doug Fisher, and Nancy Frey noted, "Good listeners are able to more accurately understand the context, tone, and intent of another person's message. How often is conflict the result of poorly delivered and understood messages? Of jumping to conclusions about others' meaning or intentions?" (2019, p. 54). Listening also doesn't stand alone. Making meaning of what one is hearing is foundational to any conversation and especially necessary when navigating disagreements.

During conversations, on occasion but especially when disagreements seem to be causing emotional responses, pause students and remind them to check if they are listening. Have them do a body check. You can say,

> Are you looking at the person who is talking? If you need to turn your head or your body right now, go ahead and do so. Is your body relaxed? If not, take a deep breath or two. Shake out your arms and hands. Think about your muscles and relaxing them.

When students feel strong emotions, they can lose sight of these behaviors, no matter how well they typically may do them. Taking a moment and reminding students will help them refocus and gives them a foundation to remember on their own, in the future.

Checking comprehension is the flip side of clarifying. When listening to others' ideas, it's important to clarify understanding (just as the speaker clarifies meaning). Asking questions and paraphrasing can bring misunderstandings to light and resolve disagreements in the same way that elaborating and rephrasing might do. Other times, checking for comprehension can bring out new disagreements even as it solidifies the initial one. That isn't automatically a bad thing. A clear understanding of the disagreement is necessary for a meaningful conversation.

Students will likely need reminders to use these skills for checking their comprehension. Adults don't always do this well during a disagreement: they make assumptions about their understanding and can feel quite confident in that understanding. If you have created anchor charts in your classroom with these skills (see Chapter 3), you can walk over to one and point at asking questions or paraphrasing to silently remind students. After a disagreement or between conversations, you can teach students that asking questions and paraphrasing are important skills for students who have not been engaged in the disagreement to try. You can tell students, "If you are hearing people disagree about something, you can step into the conversation by asking a question of one of them, or you can paraphrase what you are hearing them say." It can be helpful to hear questions or synthesis from someone who has not been actively disagreeing. This strategy also offers an option for students who may be feeling uncomfortable hearing others disagree but don't know what they can do. It gives them a strategy and some language to use.

If students are disagreeing, they are definitely doing some of the work of processing what they are hearing. Doing so respectfully and in a way that helps everyone learn is the challenge then. The sentence starters from Chapter 3 can support this practice. Students might be able to explain their disagreement respectfully by saying, "I see it differently because . . ." or "My idea is slightly different. . . ." Students need to see disagreement as an opportunity to learn together rather than a problem to overcome. After a conversation during which students disagree noticeably, ask students to reflect on how their thinking changed. Even if the students most involved in the conversation did not change their thinking at all, it is likely other students did. I often share ways students have shifted my thinking through their discussions, too. That is powerful for young children to hear: that they have taught an adult something new.

## Skills for Synthesizing Thinking

If a disagreement is going to influence learning, the participants need to synthesize their own thinking and what they are hearing from others. Like everything else about conversations, this is more challenging when a disagreement is significant. Remaining focused on the topic can be easy when people feel passionately about it, but it can also be difficult if someone is uncomfortable with disagreement and sees shifting the conversation as a way to avoid it. It is also possible that people engaged in the disagreement may not be seeing things in the same way and may not actually be focused on the exact same topic. Unless the move off topic is egregious, focusing on this is not likely the most important instructional choice you could make. If the move off topic is significant and no student brings the discussion back, you can step in and do so yourself, noting for students what you are doing.

One of the most powerful conversation skills when disagreements arise is being able to connect ideas (see Chapter 4). Finding connections between one's own ideas and those of others can ease the pain of a disagreement. Noticing agreements or similarities in thinking in the midst of disagreeing can lower the emotional temperature of the conversation. The disagreement feels less significant when it is not perceived as black-and-white. Connecting ideas can also clarify the disagreement. It can help students identify the true nature of the disagreement and not be distracted by tangential ideas.

As with asking questions and paraphrasing, students who are disagreeing or who have been listening can connect ideas. If you take a moment to pause the conversation, you can say, "If you've been listening but not really talking so far, you may have some insights that could help us in this conversation. Are you seeing ways the ideas we're hearing go together?" If no one does, you can model how you see connections between the ideas. If you aren't seeing any connections, then your students probably are not either, and it would not be a useful instructional strategy to stop and ask for that. I will admit, however, that I have been known to be surprised by connections students can make. Their perspectives are frequently not the same as mine.

## Exploring Different Perspectives

Being able to see things from another's perspective is an important skill, and essential for navigating disagreements. You can see other perspectives two different ways. The first is to consider an idea through a new lens—or **take a new angle**. The second is to **identify different views**, taking another's experiences and thoughts into consideration. Seeing other perspectives is difficult for me and for many adults. It is no less challenging for young students. That means yet another reminder for balancing the cognitive load (see Chapter 2). As you consider the strategies discussed here, think carefully about how you want students to try them and practice them. Be thoughtful about how you choose an idea or topic. Because students will not likely all share a perspective on what is good, you can focus first on seeing other perspectives using ideas and topics that are comfortable and easy for your students, like discussing whether or not a song, movie, or video game is good. As they begin to independently think things through from different perspectives (or at least consider and accept different perspectives), you can move the cognitive load to the more challenging topic or idea.

## Take a New Angle

Looking at an idea from a different angle requires being open and willing to recognize that there *are* different angles. It can be fun to help young students explore this in physical ways before trying to take it on in the metacognitive way that is needed for academic conversations. Some years ago, I took my own children to the International Spy Museum in Washington, D.C. In the museum store on our way out, we found a fun little gadget that amazed my kids. It looks like a small saltshaker, only a couple of inches tall. It has a hole on the bottom for you to look in. When you do so, you don't see what is in front of you, as you might expect. You see things off to your side. There's a small mirror inside the viewer that is angled to show you what is happening 90 degrees to one side. It takes a bit to adjust your brain to what your eye is seeing. Looking through such a viewer is surprising at first. What you expect to see and what you actually see makes you think. The viewer literally shifts your perspective. A physical demonstration like this can open a door for you to help your students understand what it means to look at something from another perspective.

Another way to do this is to **use optical illusions**. Perhaps you have seen the old/young woman image or the image of two people facing each other in which you also see a vase. Optical illusions are great fun to share with young students and can offer many of the same conversation opportunities as the viewer from the spy museum. Show students an image and ask them to take a moment to look at it without any discussion. Then allow a few students to share what they saw. Be prepared for other students to gasp in surprise when their attention is directed to something they had completely missed. Ask those students to share why they gasped. This will lead to a discussion of how something can look different when seen from a different angle or when explained in a new way.

In conversations, these ideas can come up in a couple of ways. One way gets back to the strategy of noticing and naming when students are using or approximating a skill. When you notice students looking at an idea from multiple perspectives, point it out and give students a chance to think about it and discuss what they think. I often do this when we are discussing a computation problem in math. We frequently use the math strategy of task and share (Lempp, 2017) when working on computation skills. I give 2nd grade students a problem (the "task"), such as $32 + 47 = \_\_\_$, and have them work on it independently for a period of time.

I wander the room, looking at the different strategies that students are using to solve the problem (e.g., manipulatives such as place-value blocks, number lines). When I notice students using a strategy well, especially a strategy I think their classmates might benefit from learning, I ask them if they are willing to share their work with the class. I'm looking for three to five students who will share different strategies, depending on needs and timing. Their different strategies reflect different ways of looking at the same problem or task. Some students look at the problem and want to build it with place-value blocks. Other students take a similar perspective, breaking the numbers into their place-value pieces, but don't need the blocks to do so. Still other students use a number line, looking at one of the numbers in the task as being many parts comprising one whole as they jump up the number line.

During such lessons, I notice and name how students look at the task from different perspectives. Because my students are familiar with the task-and-share strategy, they are also familiar with taking on the thinking of a peer to try a new way of tackling the same math problem. My role is helping them better understand how they have already been taking another perspective when they do this, linking what they're doing to the discussions we had about optical illusions. I might say,

> Remember how we changed our perspectives when we heard from our friends about what they saw in some of the optical illusions we looked at? Hearing someone else's thinking can help us grow our thinking. That's what you're doing here. You're seeing something, this math problem, in a different way because of how someone else explained it.

During an economics unit with 3rd graders, we read a short book about ways people make money. One of the repeated phrases in the book was about how hard it is to do the various jobs. One of my students wasn't so sure about that.

**Jason:** Why would it be hard to answer the phone? You just pick it up. That's not hard.

**Me:** That doesn't sound hard, does it? What could make answering the phone a hard job?

**Jason:** I don't know. You pick it up, you say hello, you put it down. That's not hard.

**Me:** Is that the whole thing? That's all you have to do?

**Jason:** Well, you have to talk to someone, I guess. Whoever called. My mom called the insurance company the other day with a question. She was on the phone a long time. The person had to help her. I guess that was kind of hard.

Although Jason's initial thought was completely literal (answering a phone is not hard; his 3-year-old sister can do that!), when he shifted his perspective to thinking about the job the person was actually doing, he was able to think about why it would be hard. Jason was able to see the job from another perspective.

As with other skills, it's important to model different, concrete ways to approach new ideas, questions, and problems. During our exploration of food chains, I give students a choice about sharing what they learn: They can build models or draw representations to help us think more about the topic or tell a story that illustrates how food chains operate. Through these different representations, students follow different trains of thought and questioning. When the class discusses food chains, they are in a position to share a specific perspective and to hear other perspectives. It's important to explicitly link this sharing to their thinking about optical illusions, to help them understand how the more concrete way of "seeing" different perspectives is similar to what they are doing in their thinking now. Their confidence will grow as you help them to recognize what they are doing successfully.

## Identify Different Views

Looking at an idea or question from different angles or perspectives is a helpful strategy for fresh thinking and deeper understanding. Being able to look at an idea, question, or problem from someone else's position is equally or more challenging. It is also a skill students will benefit from throughout their lives, not only in their learning but also in personal and professional relationships. One of the challenges is the tendency to make assumptions from one's own experiences and knowledge. Students tend to assume that others' lives are like theirs, that other people know the things they know and do the things they do. So, they tend to assume that other people think the way they think. They need to be open to the idea that people might have different ideas before they can see things from another's perspective.

One way to get started with this skill is to watch for students to disagree with a classmate during a conversation. Not all disagreements will lend themselves to a productive discussion of perspectives, but some definitely will. If you can find a disagreement that doesn't have a clear "right" or "wrong" answer (because some disagreements will when one student doesn't understand yet or because there isn't a right or wrong answer), then you have found a good place to start. In such a case, ask the two students to explain their perspectives and ask them to identify why they might feel differently. Perhaps their approach to problem solving is different (one needs to draw or build, and one needs to talk things through). Or perhaps they each previously learned about the same topic in different ways and that influenced their current ideas. If they can verbalize this thinking, it will give their classmates a model for different perspectives.

Jon Klassen's *I Want My Hat Back* (2011) often sparks interesting conversations with young children. In my kindergarten classroom a few years ago, my students had strong feelings about what happened in that book.

**Lina:** I couldn't believe the ending! I can't get over that! How could the bear eat that rabbit?

**Ivan:** What? No! That's not what happened! He got his hat back and the rabbit went away.

**Lina:** No way! He ate the rabbit! Didn't you hear what he said at the end?

**Ivan:** Yeah! He said he *didn't* eat the rabbit!

**Lina:** I know! He's not telling the truth! He totally ate the rabbit! That's awful!

I paused the conversation here because both Lina and Ivan felt very strongly about what they believed happened in the story. Klassen doesn't spell it out explicitly, but Lina is correct here. The bear did eat the rabbit and the reader knows this because of the way Klassen uses the dialogue to echo an earlier point in the story. This is subtle and frequently not completely understood by young students. I made the decision to focus on the disagreement rather than the text of the book. We would have plenty of opportunities to explore the text and grow as readers. This was a perfect opportunity to grow my students' skills for navigating disagreements.

**Me:** It sounds like Lina and Ivan both have strong ideas about the end of this book. Lina, you got this conversation topic started. Can you tell us about your perspective?

**Lina:** OK. The bear ate the rabbit. He wanted his hat back and the rabbit had his hat and he was mad. So, he ate the rabbit.

**Me:** Thanks, Lina. Ivan, would you like to share your perspective with us?

**Ivan:** There is no way the bear would eat the rabbit! That is just mean! He isn't mean. He just wanted his hat back. So he didn't have to eat the rabbit.

**Me:** Lina and Ivan have different perspectives on what happened in this book. They both have reasons for what they are thinking. Sometimes this happens in conversations. People have different perspectives and different ideas. Even after Lina and Ivan shared their ideas and the reasons for them, they still disagree. We aren't all going to agree all the time. Hopefully, Lina and Ivan learned from each other and the rest of us did too.

In that conversation, I was able to guide Lina and Ivan through some calmer sharing and allow everyone to see a disagreement in action. They were able to share their perspectives and help the rest of the class see how these were different and how they both had strong reasons for their beliefs. If students are unable to put their thinking into words, that is not a problem. Verbalizing one's thoughts is a challenging thing to do. You can simply point out to your students that disagreements can often stem from different perspectives. You might ask if your students can understand how one student is feeling or thinking and then if they can understand how the other student is feeling or thinking. Their ability to see both sides will give them a sense of perspectives.

Another strategy to consider is to reference other skills students have practiced and feel relatively comfortable with by this point. The skills for checking comprehension, questioning, and paraphrasing (Chapter 3) can be helpful here, and the strategies for synthesizing thinking (Chapter 4) may be worth revisiting with a few students or as a class. When students are checking their comprehension, they are taking a step toward understanding another person's perspective. To begin seeing things through someone else's eyes, the listener needs to work to understand what is being said.

In many ways, it is not possible to truly understand what others are saying without being able to see their perspective, at least to some extent. This idea is one that will help students gain confidence in their ability to see others' perspectives. By identifying what students are already doing in service of this skill, you offer them a path toward proficiency. You can support their journey on this path by noticing and naming when they are questioning and paraphrasing and taking a moment to explore what they learn from that process. Help them recognize how the work they are doing to check their comprehension supports seeing the perspective of another person.

## Using Literature to Explore Perspective

Literature is another way to explore different perspectives. One of the benefits of using books to take on difficult skills or ideas is that it is somewhat removed from students' "real world." They don't have the same emotional investment in fictional characters as they do in their own actions and those of their friends and family. This enables them to look at things with a bit of distance and be a bit more objective.

Brendan Wenzel's book, *They All Saw a Cat* (2016), is wonderful for exploring perspectives. It has minimal text, making it ideal for young learners. It is also complex in its ideas, however, which makes the story work with older elementary students as well. Throughout the book, various animals see a cat. The illustrations are all strikingly different, as the cat is depicted through the perspective of each animal. Some animals see the cat as scary. Some see it in colors or shapes that would be surprising to us, based on the way that animal's eyes work. Each perspective is unique. Each animal sees the cat in a different, individual way.

Another book with illustrations showing different perspectives is *Two Bad Ants* by Chris Van Allsburg (1988). In this book, two ants leave the others and go into a kitchen. The entire book is drawn through their perspective. The book has more text than *They All Saw a Cat* and doesn't have multiple perspectives, but seeing familiar items, like the sink and coffee maker, through the eyes of the ants is fascinating. Young children have lots to talk about through this book, discussing why things look so different to ants than to us.

Yet another resource is *The True Story of the Three Little Pigs* (Scieszka & Smith, 1996). For this book to be helpful, students must be familiar with the traditional story of the three little pigs. Jon Scieszka's retelling is from the wolf's point of view and explains what happened in a much different (and entertaining) way. Students can explore why the wolf would have such a different perspective on the story than the pigs do.

You can use several other picture-book retellings of fairy tales from different points of view in this way. Students who are familiar with specific fairy tales are often quite shaken by new perspectives on the traditional stories, but it can be a fun way to explore different perspectives. These titles are wonderful for elementary students of all ages. For a slightly more sophisticated option, check out any of Marilyn Singer's Reverso poetry collections. Reverso poems can be read from top to bottom *or* from bottom to top, with the perspective shifting depending on the choice. *Mirror, Mirror* (2010) and *Follow, Follow* (2013) are collections about fairy tales and *Echo, Echo* (2016) is full of poems about Greek myths.

Students may be able to take on the different perspectives of fictional characters more easily than they take on those of their peers. This is still a positive step and should be celebrated. Eventually—although maybe not in the time you are with these students—they will be able to do the same with the people around them. It is simply a skill that can take some time to develop and is likely one that many adults are still regularly working on. Be patient, with yourself and your students, when it comes to the skills in this chapter. Notice the ways you do (or do not) use these skills in conversations in your life, as well as how others do the same. You may find yourself quite impressed by your students and their growth as you explore these skills more deeply.

> **Sentence Starters: Seeing Other Perspectives**
>
> When I look at this from another side, it makes me think . . . .
>
> I think _____ is thinking that because . . . , which makes me think . . . .
>
> Hearing _____'s perspective has helped me understand this more. Now I'm thinking . . . .

---

Disagreeing with others is not a bad thing. Students can learn a lot from a discussion in which they are disagreeing with peers or friends. In fact, they are likely to learn more from those conversations than from ones in which everyone is in total agreement. Without the essential social-emotional skills and willingness to listen and see other perspectives, however, students are unlikely to make much progress in their learning. Developing these skills, trying them out, and growing them throughout the year will give your students a head start in lifelong learning, participating as a valuable member of a community, and being in meaningful, strong relationships. That is quite a lot to gain.

# 6

# THE PAYOFF: USING CONVERSATIONS FOR ASSESSMENT AND PLANNING

Academic conversations are powerful instructional tools, offering students opportunities to learn from their classmates and to actively process their own understandings. One of the wonderful things about academic conversations is that they also offer teachers insight into our students' learning. The conversations in which students engage open a window into their content-area and social-emotional learning. You and your students have invested a significant amount of time and energy in becoming thoughtful conversationalists, with significant payoff.

One thing you have gained is a powerful assessment tool for academic learning. The academic conversations taking place in your classroom are learning opportunities for your students, and they provide you with important data about your students' academic progress. As you listen, you can identify strengths and notice misconceptions or gaps in understanding. Conversations not only make a useful assessment tool, but also offer you information for planning future instruction. You also gain powerful student voices in your classroom. By participating in academic conversations that are student-led and developing their skills for sharing, exploring, and synthesizing thinking, your students will become willing and able to speak up and speak out.

## Assessing Content Knowledge and Skills

Although the focus throughout this book has been on developing and improving conversation skills, the end goal is not simply to have stronger conversation skills. Ultimately, you want your students to be able to use these skills to support their learning in all areas of knowledge. The stronger their conversation skills, the more likely that students will be able to use them to improve their understanding and skills in other realms. Conversations also provide opportunities to assess mastery of the topic or content that is the focus at any moment. To do this, you must decide how you want to assess content-area knowledge and what you specifically plan to assess.

### How to Assess

Making the decision about how to assess content-area knowledge and skills may be more challenging than determining how to assess conversation skills and may feel far more open-ended and broader. As you taught students the conversation skills, you assessed their mastery in this area; there has been a clear correlation between instruction and assessment. That connection may feel less certain when assessing knowledge of the content being discussed. You might also find, as you're listening to your students, that you are more focused on the conversation skills than on the topic of discussion, given all of the time and energy that has been invested in developing those skills.

At first, you may find it helpful to gather more detailed and thorough assessment data so that you keep the focus on the content rather than the discussion skills. Using a conversation map or a transcript of the conversation, as discussed in previous chapters, can allow you to review the ideas and questions about content that arose as students talked. Seeing their thoughts in black-and-white on paper (or your computer screen) can make things much clearer. Being able to read and reread student's comments—rather than just hearing them fly by during the conversation—will allow you to notice connections, misconceptions, or creative thinking that you otherwise might have missed.

The conversation mapped in Figure 6.1 collects content-area assessment information. This conversation was about a science unit on animals and their ecosystems and how humans affect them. Reviewing the conversation map, I noted two big ideas that came up regularly: (1) things that are the same and things that are different for humans and other animals and (2) the need humans have for animals. Those are big, important ideas in this unit, and I was glad to see them pop up often. Reflecting on this conversation also helped me realize that the next step for my students was to explore what humans should be doing the same or doing differently, now that they were aware of and thinking about those big ideas. I planned that for future lessons and conversations.

As you begin to feel more comfortable collecting assessment information from classroom conversations, you can begin collecting data using quicker, simpler approaches. For example, if students are discussing what is and is not a cycle in nature, you might make quick notes on a class chart about students' level of understanding. Each time students share their thinking or ask a question, mark a symbol or number to represent how well they seem to understand

154  Demystifying Discussion

FIGURE 6.1 | **CONVERSATION MAP: ASSESSING CONTENT KNOWLEDGE**

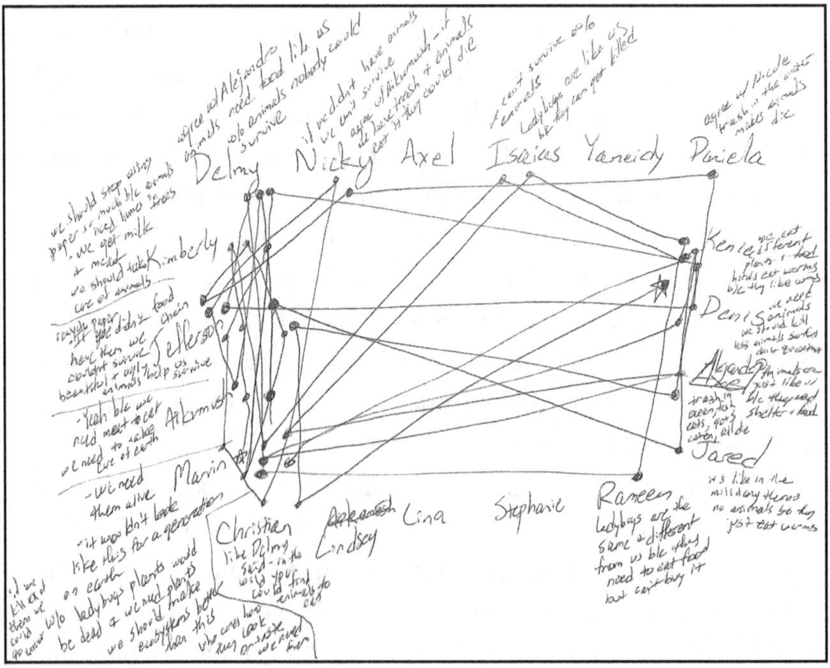

natural cycles. A 1 or a minus sign might mean that student has limited understanding, whereas a 2 or a plus sign would represent some facility with the ideas and a 3 or plus sign with a circle around it shows a student's strong comprehension. Using a minus sign, a plus sign, and a circled plus sign also allows you to just add to previous markings as students demonstrate evolving and stronger comprehension through their conversations, rather than having to change the marking each time. (At the first glimmer of knowledge, you write the minus sign; when the student continues to show strength, you make this symbol a plus sign, and then add a circle if warranted.) If there is no marking, you will know that student did not actively contribute to the conversation in a way that showed understanding.

When using a chart like this (see Figure 6.2), it's helpful to include a space for noting any contributions that stand out, such as comments or questions that are especially insightful or provocative or ideas that reflect common misconceptions or errors. Anything that is at one extreme can be worth recording for future use. You can revisit these ideas at the end of the conversation or in a future lesson for discussion or evaluation by the students. Exploring their own ideas more deeply invites students to take ownership over their thinking and learning.

FIGURE 6.2 | **CHARTING COMPREHENSION: ASSESSING CONTENT KNOWLEDGE**

| Student | Understands that a cycle is a pattern | Understands that a cycle repeats | Notes |
|---|---|---|---|
| Angie | — | | |
| Damien | + | + | |
| Luci | + | ⊕ | "I know we breathe in oxygen that we get from plants. Is there a cycle in that?" |

Figure 6.2 shows that Angie either said very little or that her understanding about cycles is still developing. I may want to use another assessment tool or have a quick conversation with her to gather more data on her level of understanding. Damien and Luci spoke more frequently and showed relatively strong levels of understanding about cycles. Luci's comment about breathing oxygen was one I wanted to remember when considering future instruction.

Just as when you're assessing conversation skills, consider the assessment routines and strategies you already have in place. If you have ways you take anecdotal notes during lessons, try that during an academic conversation or two. If you have charts or lists that work for you, adapt them to use in this area. Some of your routines will work for you immediately, whereas others will require some tweaking to fit what you want to glean from your students' discussions. Sometimes, your existing assessment tools won't work at all for assessing content-area knowledge through student conversations, and you'll have to try something new. What matters is that you determine what methods are meaningful for you as well as being doable—both of these are required criterion, or you are not likely to stick with them.

## What to Assess

Deciding what to assess may be straightforward or it may be more complex. The prompt or topic for the discussion should play a large role in your planning. Sometimes you might present a prompt or question that is specific and immediately focuses the discussion. Other times, you may opt to have the conversation topic you present to students be broad and open-ended, allowing for them to make more choices in the direction of the conversation. Figure 6.3 provides examples of both types of prompts, in different content areas.

The prompt you offer for a conversation significantly affects how your students discuss a concept. If the idea is still a fairly new one for your students, you may want to offer a more targeted prompt; this will help them focus and get started in a conversation. When students have had lots of time and experience with an idea, your prompt may be broader and more creative, offering them opportunities to demonstrate understanding in more unusual ways and to explore new ways of thinking about a topic. Consider the prompts in Figure 6.3 about 2-D and 3-D shapes, for example. Asking students how 2-D and 3-D shapes are related focuses their thinking. Asking them to use what they know about 2-D and 3-D shapes to theorize about 1-D is a more creative angle that uses the same knowledge.

Similarly, if you have a specific standard or bit of knowledge within a unit that you want to assess, give students a question or prompt that will push them hard in that direction. (You can't

FIGURE 6.3 | **EXAMPLES OF SPECIFIC AND OPEN-ENDED PROMPTS**

| Content Area | Prompts |
| --- | --- |
| English/Language Arts | • How did Mia and her grandmother change each other? (After reading Meg Medina's *Mango, Abuela, and Me*, 2015)<br>• What did you learn about friendship from this book? (After reading Jacqueline Woodson's *Each Kindness*, 2012)<br>• What are you thinking about [the book]? (For a more general response) |
| Mathematics | • Does the order of numbers matter when you add or subtract?<br>• How are multiplication and division similar? How are they different?<br>• How are 2-D and 3-D shapes related?<br>• Given what you know about 2-D and 3-D shapes, what could 1-D (4-D) be?<br>• What makes math challenging for you? |
| Science | • If an alien showed up on Earth, how would you explain why there are shadows?<br>• Which natural disaster would be the most dangerous? Why?<br>• Could we live on the moon? Why or why not? |
| Social Studies | • Should kindergartners at our school dress up as Native Americans and Pilgrims for Thanksgiving?<br>• Would you have wanted to live in ancient Egypt? Why do you feel that way?<br>• Which of the school rules do you think is the most important, and why? |

completely control their conversations, but you can start them down a certain street.) For example, during a geometry unit, you may want to determine how well students understand the characteristics of a square. You could ask something as clear as "What makes a square a square?" Or you could offer them several images (some squares and some similar shapes) and have them discuss how they could prove which ones are and are not squares. These prompts will set you up to assess students' understanding of the characteristics of a square.

If you are aiming for a broader conversation, rethink your prompt a bit. Let's say you want to explore students' understanding of fractions and decimals and the relationship between the two. Again, you could begin the conversation with a basic question such as "What is the relationship between a fraction and a decimal?" Or you might ask students, "Can all fractions be decimals? Can all decimals be fractions?" Another option would be to show a picture of a fractional piece, or some whole pieces and a fractional piece, and ask, "Is this a fraction? Is this a decimal? How do you know?" The way you present the question or idea will affect how directly and specifically students talk about the topic. When planning for conversations, decide how much you want to direct the conversation to a specific idea or how much you want to leave it open to interpretation and different possible journeys.

Whether you decide to give students a laser focus or set them up with a wide-open topic, you can use the conversation to watch for misconceptions or gaps in student learning. Here, anticipating and knowing what common misconceptions or gaps in understanding are, especially for the age of your students, will make it easier to assess. Knowing what to look for is helpful, whether it is looking for strengths or for areas of need. The possible pitfall, however, is that you might not notice other misconceptions or errors if you are too focused on specific ones. Students can be quite surprising in ways that are enlightening. This could be simply that you are on the lookout for misconceptions or errors that come from students working to understand more sophisticated ideas, when instead, their misconceptions and errors come from prior understanding.

This has happened when exploring fractions with upper elementary students. I'm looking for misconceptions about how to add, subtract, multiply, or divide fractions and then realize that some students still do not truly understand what the denominator signifies. In my search to be sure students understand the computation, I could easily miss this more basic confusion. Be prepared and open-minded. You never know what insights you might gain as you listen.

## Planning Future Instruction

I find it enlightening to review assessment data I have collected to determine what my students truly understand about our unit of study and where they might have misconceptions or gaps in understanding, and it pushes me forward. It is exciting to identify the strengths my students show and to see them in such an authentic setting as a conversation. Many times, I have noticed misconceptions and gaps that surprised me. Those surprises are a positive for me, too; I wouldn't want that information to slip through the cracks.

As with any assessment information, you'll use what you gain from students' academic conversations to plan for future instruction. When students have not mastered a concept or idea, one question to ask is "Do I really need to reteach this?" Is this something your students must know right now, or is it something you will be returning to in the future? If the latter, perhaps you should file this information away for that time. If content does need to be retaught immediately, what is the best way to do so? How many students still need more help in this area?

### Identifying Strengths and Misconceptions

When, during a conversation, you identify key understanding, you need to determine how widespread that is. Did one student make an insightful comment, while the rest of the class did not seem to follow? Or were many students supporting one another's thinking about the topic? I have often fallen into the trap of believing that one or two students' clear understanding of an idea was a sign that my whole class had gotten it. A single academic conversation is not going to give you a window into every student's level of mastery with a specific topic, but it can be a guide. If only one or two students seem to have a deep understanding, you might enlist their help for future instruction. They may have ideas or ways of explaining the topic that will connect with their classmates. In future instruction or conversations, those students with strong understandings can use the skills for clarifying their thinking, from Chapter 2, to explain to and teach their peers. If many students are talking knowledgeably about the topic, you may be ready to move on in your instruction.

Similarly, when you notice misconceptions or gaps in understanding, you need to decide if this is limited to a few students or if it is a concern across the class. If you identify when a student is stating a common misconception, you can scan the other students to see if they seem comfortable with that statement or if it seems to bother them. The more comfortable they seem, the more likely it is that they share that misconception.

In one conversation in my 3rd grade classroom, a student said, "If the numerators are the same, then you look at the denominator to decide which fraction is bigger. If the denominator is smaller, then the fraction is smaller." As I looked around at my students, I saw most of them nodding in agreement. That told me we needed to spend more time exploring fractions, especially looking at what happens when just the numerator or just the denominator changes. If most students had disagreed, I would have planned some small-group time with those who seemed to share this misconception.

Reflecting on one conversation map (see Figure 6.1), I noticed that multiple students discussed a couple of important, big ideas.

Quite a few students referenced ways that humans need animals. Seeing how many students talked about that idea, in a variety of ways, told me that my class had a solid understanding of it. We could begin building on that idea. A few students also talked about ways that humans and other animals were similar and different. That big idea did not come up as frequently, so I felt less confident that it was widespread. In the class chart about cycles (Figure 6.2), Luci mentioned a cycle with oxygen from plants. She did not seem completely certain about it, and it was a cycle we had not explored in class. My students did not need to know about that cycle, but it is an interesting one in nature, and once Luci had introduced it, I had the option to follow up. Her reference to it suggested that there might be some background knowledge we could build on, at least for some students, to extend their understanding of cycles.

## Extending and Reteaching

Misconceptions or gaps in understanding that show themselves during conversations are helpful guides. When you have identified one or more, you can plan how to address them. One of the first questions is whether you should plan for small-group support or more whole-class instruction in that area. You might need more information to make that decision. Using exit tickets focused on the specific idea at the heart of the misconception will give you an idea of the scope of the misconception. If you decide the need is for small-group instruction, there are more options to consider. You can work with small groups of students who need more support to master the content and reteach. Another option is to plan for more heterogeneous groups, combining students who showed strong understanding with students who need more support. Such groups could have further discussion on the topic, with students who are ready leading the way and guiding their classmates to stronger understandings. Conversations serve not only as assessment tools, but also as learning opportunities for everyone (Michaels & O'Connor, 2012).

If you determine the need is more widespread and should be addressed as a whole class, how are you going to reteach the topic? You can plan activities, books, or other lessons to address any misconceptions you have noted—or you might consider how to use more classroom conversations. When I noticed, in a conversation, that my students did not understand that a square was a special kind of rectangle, I planned another conversation. For this conversation, I supplied my students with images and manipulatives of rectangles and squares. The prompt I gave them was to sort the shapes and then define what makes something a rectangle and what makes something a square. This activity scaffolded their thinking about the shapes while still allowing them to discuss and co-create their understanding.

It is also possible that a classroom conversation will suggest that your students, all or some of them, are ready for something new. You might be ready to move on from a certain unit or standard, or perhaps this is an opportunity for enrichment. I made the latter choice following my class's discussion about cycles. Luci's comment pushed us in a direction that was not in our grade-level standards but definitely supported students' learning. Her comment got us started on some research about the cycle of oxygen and carbon dioxide. Just as with reteaching, any extension you identify may be for the whole class or small groups of students who would benefit.

The more frequently your students engage in academic conversations, the easier it will be for you to plan for these and use them as instructional and assessment tools. Checklists and rubrics may be helpful, or you may find yourself needing these less and less. As you grow comfortable listening to your students and noting the strengths they demonstrate and the needs they show through their talk, you can begin modifying your strategies for collecting data. A few notes might be enough for you to plan for future instruction and address what you are noting. Again, you will determine what tools and strategies will be the most useful to you. Identify ways that are efficient—because inefficient strategies will be cumbersome and fall by the wayside—and that yield meaningful information. It might be setting up a spreadsheet to collect data or it might be a chart to take notes on that lists your students' names.

The data collection strategies you use in other areas can inform how you collect data during conversations. The goal is to gather information that informs how well your students are using the conversation skills or how well they understand the content they are discussing. One last reminder: Don't forget the power of student self-assessments. Don't underestimate what your students' reflections on their learning and skills also can tell you.

## Taking Time and Having Patience

Collecting data and making meaning of it may seem overwhelming, especially when you consider the variety of information you want or are trying to collect and all the ways you could use it. Baby steps are totally reasonable. Pick one way to collect data and do only that until it feels easy for you. If you want to start with a chart of your students' names, on which you put a check every time they speak, then do so. If you're feeling a bit more confident and you want to use that chart to mark when students demonstrate a specific skill (e.g., paraphrasing; see Chapter 3), then start there.

When students are taking on something new, it will not look perfect immediately. They will approximate the skill as they develop facility with it. The same is true for teachers. It takes time for anyone to become proficient with something new. Show yourself some grace and give yourself permission to try and to fail... and to try some more. Don't let the expectation of perfection hold you back from trying.

Similarly, remember that the way you collect assessment data will not always look the same. For many years now, I have been keeping running records when my students read aloud, noting their fluency and any errors they make. I use a set structure, with specific notations that fit (for me). My running records look similar, but if I am looking for a certain skill or noticing a student's specific challenge, I adapt my running record for that focus. The same holds true here.

In the conversation map in Figure 6.1, for example, my focus was on how well my students were building on one another's ideas; I did not need to capture everything they said in the conversation. I focused on capturing the ways they demonstrated that they were building on others' ideas, by agreeing or disagreeing and supporting their thinking. Knowing I didn't need to write down everything and accepting that I may have missed a line or two between students made collecting this assessment information less stressful. I wasn't ready to do this when I first began mapping conversations. It took practice with the tool to be able to be flexible with it. Figure 6.4 is a conversation map that shows who spoke during this discussion. It does not record all details of what these students said, but it does illustrate who was agreeing, disagreeing, and supporting those statements.

Teaching and learning is a powerful cycle, and efficient and meaningful assessment information makes that cycle work to the best of its ability. You teach your students skills and ideas, and they practice them. Observing that practice, through their conversations, helps you analyze their strengths and needs. From there, you return to the teaching—either reteaching as needed or moving forward as students are ready. The cycle continues, teaching and learning together.

FIGURE 6.4 | **CONVERSATION MAP: FOCUSING ON A SKILL**

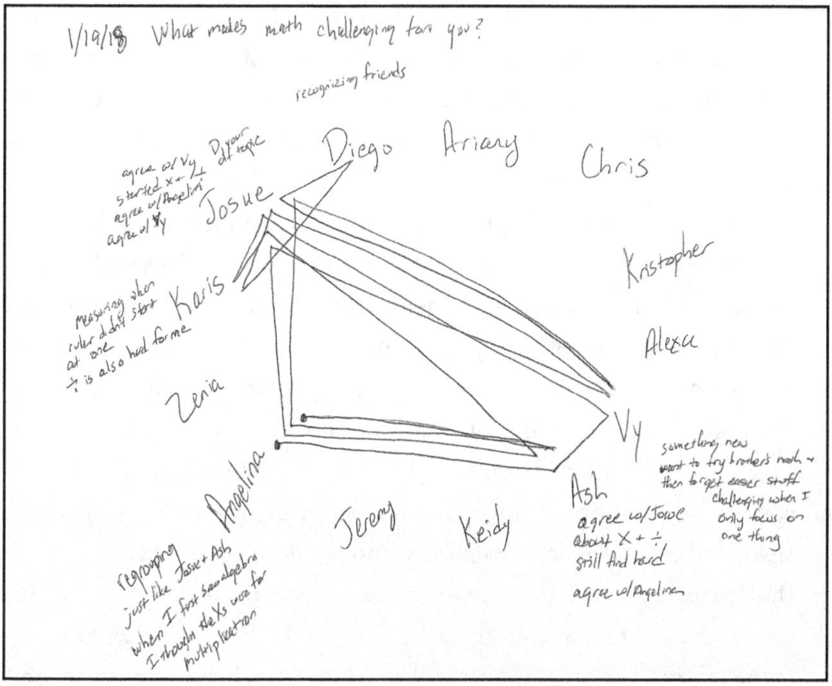

1/19/18  What makes math challenging for you?

recognizing friends

agree w/ Vy   Different people
started X + ÷
agree w/ Angelina
agree w/ Vy

Diego   Ariany   Chris

Josue

Kristopher

measuring when
ruler didn't start
at one
÷ is also hard for me

Karis

Alexa

Zenia

Vy

something new
want to try brother's math +
then forget easier stuff
challenging when I
only focus on
one thing

Angelina

Ash

agree w/ Josue
about X + ÷
still find hard
agree w/ Angelina

regrouping
just like Josue + Ash
when I first saw algebra
I thought the Xs was for
multiplication

Jeremy   Keidy

# Empowering Student Voice

In research on descriptive feedback, Carol Rodgers noted that "there were signs that students were capable of reflecting on and expressing what they actually learned and looking to their own experience for verification" (2018, p. 95) Although this comment is not explicitly about academic conversations, the idea is the same. When students have the opportunity to engage in meaningful ways about their own learning, they will show what they have learned and continue their learning. Being a part of classroom conversations in which they learn from their peers and add to their peers' knowledge helps students to recognize their own power and agency. I have watched young students grow their conversation skills throughout a school year; I have seen their confidence and self-esteem grow, too. Their belief in the value of what they have to say gives students the authority to speak more and more frequently.

Years ago, in my 1st grade classroom, I stopped assigning seats and moved to flexible seating, with tables of various sizes and heights as well as a couch and lots of beanbags, pillows, and other options. Students chose where they wanted to work at any given moment. I was nervous about this decision but jumped in anyway. At the start of the year, we had conversations about how to decide on a good place to work and when you might want to make a change. If necessary, I told students to move, but that was fairly rare. They were quite responsible with their decisions about where to work. The thing that surprised me most was how this move shifted the way my students saw our classroom. It was no longer *my* classroom where they came every day. It was now *our* classroom. This became clear when I realized they were using spaces in the room that I had not intended for them, such as a desk I had provided for a student teacher who was scheduled to start in a few weeks. If the desk was there and unoccupied, my students saw it as a possible place to work.

This is what you'll see with student voice, as well. At first, it may take time for all students to participate in classroom conversations. Over time, however, students will share their thinking outside those conversations. They will realize they can and should speak. Your responses to the classroom conversations, the way you have noticed and named, the celebrations you have had for students' successes, the plans you have designed based on what students said in previous discussions—all of these things are signs to your young students that what they have to say is important.

As Russell Quaglia and Michael J. Corso wrote,

> Although the world of education seems obsessed with testing at the moment, most students are not similarly preoccupied. Rather, *students want to feel like they matter to their teachers and school leaders as a person*, not just as a test score. (2014, p. 32, emphasis added)

Students know they matter when others—teachers and peers—are listening to them. Classroom conversations play a significant role in this.

---

The COVID-19 pandemic and the ways it affected schools, virtual learning, and social distancing in person have reminded many of us of the social nature of human beings. Being physically apart for so long, we looked for other ways to interact and connect. That need for connection is part of being human. Those connections are not only crucial for our well-being but also a significant part of learning and developing.

Conversations play an important role in connecting us and in helping us learn. The ability to engage in meaningful, respectful, and productive discussions with family, friends, and peers is a skill that will serve students at least as well as the skills they are developing as readers, writers, and mathematicians. And, like those skills, we can teach our students to be better conversationalists, and we can help them learn to use skills independently and to great advantage. Not only will they benefit as individuals, but also we, as a society, will benefit from citizens who have developed the ability to listen to and talk with others.

# ACKNOWLEDGMENTS

I grew up as a teacher at Annandale Terrace Elementary School in Fairfax County, Virginia—the best gift I could ever have been given. Mary Ann Ryan hired me as a brand-new teacher, and getting that job is still one of my greatest professional accomplishments. She offered me thoughtful professional development and leadership opportunities I'm sure I hadn't earned.

Chris Dickens and Andrea Garris continued to spoil me for all future administrators by offering teachers the respect we deserved as professionals and ensuring we had the resources we needed to serve our students and their families. Every conversation in that building felt like strong professional development because of the brilliance and thoughtfulness of the staff.

I couldn't have had better teachers and colleagues than Amy Greene, Jennifer Kalletta, Charlene O'Brien, Ann-Bailey Lipsett, Catherine Weiss, and Melissa Fleischer. Judy Stokes was my mentor as a new teacher, and I would likely not still be teaching if she hadn't been there those first few years. Kasey Cain has been a colleague and long-time friend, and her contributions to my understanding of social-emotional learning improved this book, as well as the experiences my students have now and in the future.

This work consciously began for me when I was teaching at Lynbrook Elementary School. Cathy Podagrosi offered to lead some conversations with my 3rd grade students about books. It opened my eyes to the possibilities. I will be forever grateful to Jessie Duvel and Anthony Ramakis, who spent a lot of time recording and transcribing conversations and analyzing them with me; to my teammates Megan Kratz and Taylor Heil, who set high standards for our students and ourselves and made it possible for this work to go deeper than I would ever have dreamed; and to Jay Nocco, Debbie Diaz-Arnold, and Erika Aspuria, administrators who never saw our students, English language learners, as anything less than brilliant—and made sure we all did the same.

When I was new to Fort Belvoir Primary, Megan Shifflet and Kristin Emory immediately were on board with engaging students in academic conversations. Both of these phenomenal instructional coaches helped me try things in my classroom, reflect, and plan. Their ideas and generosity made a huge difference in my teaching.

ASCD's Emerging Leaders program has been a journey in all the best ways. The stops along the way have included conference presentations on the topic of academic conversations; long discussions with inspiring educators from around the world; and introductions to new people, ideas, and resources. This opportunity has been one of the most significant of my teaching career; it has affected me deeply and broadly and continues to open up new and often unexpected avenues.

As a result of that program, I met Allison Scott, a senior acquisitions editor at ASCD. When she first suggested I think about writing a book, it was flattering but seemed absurd. She kept asking. She'd deserve my immense thanks just for that alone; working with her as an editor to develop this book increases my gratitude exponentially. I not only firmly believe that her suggestions and thoughts made this book far better than it would have been, but also am confident she made me a far better writer than I was when I began. The entire editorial staff at ASCD has done so much for me and for education in general through their work, and I am grateful I've had the chance to work with them.

Similarly, the Northern Virginia Writing Project made for a life-changing summer some years ago. I wasn't convinced then that I was a writer, but the Summer Institute and the teachers I met there pushed me further along that path. Seeing those classroom teachers write, professionally and personally, was eye-opening for me. It was proof that such things could be done. The people there believed I could be one of them, which felt a bit like a miracle.

One person deserves a special thank-you. Dahlia Constantine has been a friend, practically a sister, almost since I first met her. She has encouraged me, supported me, validated me, and cared for me through professional and personal challenges. Sometimes I look at the people in my life and think I must be doing something right if these are my friends. Dahlia is that for me all of the time.

I am surrounded by educators in my family—aunts and uncles and cousins in various states and countries, doing all kinds of work in education. This may be why I always knew I wanted to be a teacher. Although neither my parents nor my sister are in education (my nurse mother did spend some time developing nursing curriculum and teaching nursing students), they listen to my stories, encourage me when I'm feeling low, and generally make me feel like a rock star educator. They've also taught me to be a better teacher and better person, even having had no pedagogical training. They're just that wise.

My own two children, Kate and Charlie, seem to have always known they are writers. I think it is highly possible that, as teenagers, they've written more words in their lives than I have in mine. It is thrilling to see the stories they tell and lessons they impart. I can only begin to imagine what more they will write in the future. I have no doubt they can write anything they want into existence and definitely write their own deliverance.

My husband, Jeff, wrote a book a decade ago. At the time I could not imagine doing what he had done. I saw what it took. It seemed beyond me. His belief in me and support of me are a huge part of what convinced me this was possible. His encouragement throughout the process kept me going. It is a cliché, but I also know it to be true, that this would not have happened without him.

# REFERENCES

Alexander, R. (2018). Developing dialogic teaching: Genesis, process, trial. *Research Papers in Education. 33*(5), 561–598.

Barron, L., & Kinney, P. (2021). We Belong: 50 Strategies to Create Community and Revolutionize Classroom Management. ASCD.

Beaty, D., & Collier, B. (2013). *Knock, knock: My dad's dream for me.* Little, Brown.

Berger, G., & Berger, M. (2010). *True or false: Planets.* Scholastic.

Boaler, J. (n.d.). *Mistakes grow your brain.* Youcubed. https://www.youcubed.org/evidence/mistakes-grow-brain/

Boaler, J., & Anderson, R. (2018). Considering the rights of learners in classrooms: The importance of mistakes and growth assessment practices. *Democracy and Education, 26*(2), 7.

Board of Education, Commonwealth of Virginia. (2002). *English standards of learning for Virginia public schools.* https://www.doe.virginia.gov

Buckley, M. A. (2015). *Sharing the blue crayon: How to integrate social, emotional, and literacy learning.* Stenhouse.

Bunting, E. (1997). *A day's work.* Clarion.

Canetti, Y. (1999). *Our world of wonders.* Steck-Vaughn.

CASEL. (2020). CASEL's *SEL Framework: What are the core competence areas and where are they promoted?* https://casel.org/wp-content/uploads/2020/12/CASEL-SEL-Framework-11.2020.pdf

CASEL. (2021a). Personal SEL Reflection. https://schoolguide.casel.org/resource/adult-sel-self-assessment/

CASEL. (2021b). *SEL: What are the core competence areas and where are they promoted?* https://casel.org/sel-framework/

Centers for Disease Control and Prevention (CDC). (2021). *Data and statistics on children's mental health.* https://www.cdc.gov/childrensmentalhealth/data.html

Clark, A.-M., Anderson, R. C., Kuo, L.-J., & Kim, I-H. (2003). Collaborative reasoning: Expanding ways for children to talk and think in school. *Educational Psychology Review, 15*(2), 181–198. https://doi.org/10.1023/A:1023429215151

Copeland, L. A. (1998). *Hunter and his amazing remote control.* Youthlight.

Eisenberg, A. R. (1987). Learning to argue with parents and peers. *Argumentation, 1,* 113–125. https://doi.org/10.1007/BF00182256

Fisher, D., Frey, N., & Rothenberg, C. (2008). *Content-area conversations: How to plan discussion-based lessons for diverse language learners.* ASCD.

Fleenor, M. (2010). *Responding to student questions when you don't know the answer.* Faculty Focus. https://www.facultyfocus.com/articles/teaching-and-learning/responding-to-student-questions-when-you-dont-know-the-answer/

Hattie, J. (2012). *Visible learning for teachers: Maximizing impact on learning.* Routledge.

Heard, G., & McDonough, J. (2009). *A place for wonder: Reading and writing nonfiction in the primary grades.* Stenhouse.

Jerald, C. D. (2009). *Defining a 21st century education.* Center for Public Education. http://www.centerforpubliceducation.org/Learn-About/21st-Century/Defining-a-21st-Century-Education-Full-Report-PDF.pdf

Klassen, J. (2011). *I want my hat back.* Candlewick Press.

Lê, M., & Santat, D. (2018) *Drawn together.* Little, Brown.

Lempp, J. (2017). *Math workshop: Five steps to implementing guided math, learning stations, reflection, and more, grades K–6.* Math Solutions.

Lukoff, K. (2019). *When Aidan became a brother.* Lee & Low Books.

Medina, M., & Dominguez, A. (2015). *Mango, Abuela, and me.* Candlewick Press.

Mehan, H. (1979). *Learning lessons: social organization in the classroom.* Harvard University Press. https://doi.org/10.4159/harvard.9780674420106

Michaels, S., & O'Connor, C. (2012). *Talk science primer.* TERC.

Miranda, L.-M., Lacamoire, A., & Chernow, R. (2016). *Hamilton: An American musical* [Vocal selections]. Warner/Chappell.

Mooney, C. G. (2000). *Theories of childhood: An introduction to Dewey, Montessori, Erikson, Piaget, and Vygotsky.* Redleaf Press.

National Council of Teachers of English. (1996). *NCTE/IRA standards for the English language arts.* https://ncte.org/resources/standards/ncte-ira-standards-for-the-english-language-arts/

National Governors Association Center for Best Practices, Council of Chief State School Officers. (2010). *Common core state standards for English language arts.* http://www.corestandards.org

Quaglia, R. J., & Corso, M. J. (2014). *Student voice: The instrument of change.* Corwin.

Resnick, L. B., Asterhan, C. S., & Clarke, S. N. (2018). *Accountable talk: Instructional dialogue that builds the mind.* Geneva, Switzerland: International Academy of Education (IAE) and International Bureau of Education (IBE) of the United Nations Educational, Scientific and Cultural Organization (UNESCO).

Responsive Classroom. (2016, June). *What is morning meeting?* https://www.responsiveclassroom.org/what-is-morning-meeting/

Rodgers, C. (2018). Descriptive feedback: Student voice in K–5 classrooms. *Australian Educational Researcher, 45,* 87–102. https://doi.org/10.1007/s13384-018-0263-1

Scieszka, J., & Smith, L. (1996). *The true story of the three little pigs.* Puffin Books.

Siegel, D. J., & Bryson, T. P. (2011). *The whole-brain child: 12 proven strategies to nurture your child's developing mind.* Robinson.

Singer, M. (2010). *Mirror, mirror: A book of reverso poems.* Dutton Books for Young Readers.

Singer, M. (2013). *Follow, follow: A book of reverso poems.* Dial Books.

Singer, M. (2016). *Echo, echo: Reverso poems about Greek myths.* Dial Books.

Smith, D., Fisher, D. B., & Frey, N. (2015). *Better than carrots and sticks: Restorative practices for positive classroom management.* ASCD.

Smith, D., Fisher, D. B., & Frey, N. (2019). *All learning is social and emotional: Helping students develop essential skills for the classroom and beyond.* ASCD.

Spies, T. G., & Xu, Y. (2018). Scaffolded academic conversations: Access to 21st-century collaboration and communication skills. *Intervention in School and Clinic, 54*(1), 22–30.

Sprenger, M. (2020). *Social-emotional learning and the brain: Strategies to help your students thrive.* ASCD.

Stone, T. L. (2013). *Who says women can't be doctors? The story of Elizabeth Blackwell.* Macmillan.

Texas Education Agency. (2010). *Texas essential knowledge and skills for English language arts and reading.* https://tea.texas.gov

Tomlinson, C. A. (2014). *The differentiated classroom: Responding to the needs of all learners.* ASCD.

Van Allsburg, C. (1988). *Two bad ants.* HMH Books for Young Readers.

Vygotsky, L. S. (1978). *Mind in society: The development of higher psychological processes.* Harvard University Press.

Walsh, J. A., & Sattes, B. D. (2015). *Questioning for classroom discussion: Purposeful speaking, engaged listening, deep thinking.* ASCD.

Weinstein, R. S., Marshall, H. H., Brattesani, K. A., & Middlestadt, S. E. (1982). Student perceptions of differential teacher treatment in open and traditional classrooms. *Journal of Educational Psychology, 74*(5), 678.

Wenzel, B. (2016). *They all saw a cat.* Chronicle Books.

West, L., & Cameron, A. (2013). *Turn and talk: One powerful practice, so many uses.* Metamorphosis Teaching Learning Communities. Retrieved from https://ev4ngelf.files.wordpress.com/2014/09/turn-and-talk.pdf

Willems, M. (2006). *Don't let the pigeon stay up late.* Hyperion.

Woodson, J. (2012). *Each kindness.* Nancy Paulsen Books.

# INDEX

The letter *f* following a page number denotes a figure.

academic content, balanced with conversational skills, 4–5, 44–46, 74–75, 86, 104–105, 141
academic conversations. *See* conversations
academic standards, 7, 90
active listening, 74–75
adding *because*, to support ideas, 57–58, 136
"adding on," 92–95
agreeing, 91–92. *See also* disagreements
*All Learning Is Social and Emotional* (Smith, Fisher and Frey), 30
analysis. *See* processing skills
anchor charts, 138–139
anxiety, 35–37
argumentation contrasted with arguing, 127
assessment. *See also* charts and checklists
   clarification of thoughts, 68
   of comprehension, 88–89
   connections between ideas, 115–116, 115*f*

assessment. *See also* charts and checklists (*continued*)
   content-area, 153–159
   conversations as assessment tool, 151–153
   focus on topic, 109–110
   inclusion of peers, 122–124
   initiation of conversation, 54–56
   inviting others in, 122–123
   of listening skills, 77–78
   of processing skills, 95–96
   self-assessment by students, 59–60, 109–110
   of students' skills, 42–43
   supporting ideas, 59–61
   targeted prompts, 156–159

Barron, Laurie, 33
*because*, to support ideas, 57–58, 136
Bell Game, 117–118
benefits for students, of conversations, 1–2, 6, 8–9
Boaler, Jo, 22
body check for awareness, 138
body language, 74, 119–120

# Index

books, to explore differing perspectives, 148–150
Buckley, Mary Anne, 18

Cameron, Antonia, 127
CASEL. *See* Collaborative for Academic, Social, and Emotional Learning (CASEL)
changing one's mind, 124
charts and checklists. *See also* data collection
    anchor charts, 138–139
    for assessment of comprehension, 155*f*
    for assessment of inviting others in, 122–123
    checklist for initiation of conversation, 55*f*
    to reinforce listening skills, 75, 138–139
    rubric for assessing idea connections, 115–116, 115*f*
    for self-awareness and self-management skills, 32
civil discourse, 37–39
clarification of thoughts, skills for, 61–70, 136–137
classroom management. *See also* morning meetings and "share time"
    control, relinquishing, 13, 15–17
    "mistakes friendly" classrooms, 22
    physical space, 16–17
    routine and structure, 34–35
    seating arrangements, 166
cognitive load, balancing, 4–5, 44–46, 74–75, 86, 104–105, 141
Collaborative for Academic, Social and Emotional Learning (CASEL), 9, 30–31, 101, 128. *See also* social-emotional skills
Common Core State Standards, 90
community, classroom as, 13, 20, 33, 133, 166
compassion and empathy, 133–134
comprehension tools
    chart to track assessment of, 155*f*

comprehension tools (*continued*)
    paraphrasing, 85–87
    questions for clarification, 82–85
    questions for information, 79–82
    skills for checking, 138–139
connections
    assessing connections, 115*f*
    between ideas, 110–116
    importance of, for learning, 1
    as tool during disagreements, 140
content-area assessments, 153–159
control, relinquishing, 13, 15–17
conversational transcripts, 153
conversation maps, 68–70, 69*f*, 96*f*, 107, 153, 154*f*, 164–165, 165*f*
conversation prompts, 156–157
conversations
    as assessment tool, 151–153
    benefits of, 1–2, 6, 8–9
    challenges for younger students, 9–10
    initiation of, 46–56
    participants, 41
    purpose and goals, 42–44
    topics, 42
    unprompted conversations, 104–105
conversation summary sample, 108*f*
Copeland, Lori Ann, 32
Corso, Michael J., 166–167
counselors, school, 101–102
COVID-19 pandemic, 167
curiosity, 25–27

data collection, 162–164
decision making, responsible, 33–34, 135
defending ideas. *See* supporting ideas
defining, to clarify thoughts, 65–67
digressions. *See* focus on topic
disagreements. *See also* perspectives, differing
    agreeing and disagreeing, 91–92
    argumentation contrasted with arguing, 127
    background information about, 126–129

disagreements. *See also* perspectives, differing (*continued*)
 and sharing one's thinking, 136–137
 and Social-Emotional competencies, 129–135
drawing, as planning tool for students, 51–52

*Echo, Echo* (Singer), 149
Eisenberg. Ann R., 128
elaborating, to clarify thoughts, 61–64, 136
emojis, 60
emotional responses, 127–128, 130
empathy and compassion, 133–134
engaged listening, 73–75
enrichment and extension of curriculum, 162
examples and nonexamples of conversational skills, 75–76. *See also* sample conversations

facial expressions, 74, 119–120
feelings, awareness of, 32–33
fictional characters, as examples, 133
Fisher, Douglas (Doug), 30, 137
"fist of five," 109–110
focus on topic
 assessment of, 109–110
 building self-awareness, 101–103
 noticing moves off topic, 103–106
 returning to topic, 106–109
*Follow, Follow* (Singer), 149
Frey, Nancy, 30, 137
future instruction, planning, 159–163

games to promote impulse control, 117–118

*Hunter and His Amazing Remote Control* (Copeland), 32, 131

ideas, sharing others', 76–77
impulse control, 101–102, 117–118
inclusion of peers, 116–124

initiation of conversation
 asking questions, 47–51
 assessment of, 54–56
 new ideas, introducing, 52–54
 presenting ideas, 46–47
 writing and drawing to plan, 51–52
International Reading Association, 7
IRE model (initiation, response, evaluation), 14, 25, 47–48, 72

Kinney, Patti, 33

lifelong learning skills, 30, 43
listening skills, 73–78, 137–139
literature, as classroom tool, 133, 148–150
Lukoff, Kyle, 107

math skills, 23–24, 142–143
media examples as teaching tool, 76, 120
metacognition, 97–98, 109
*Mirror, Mirror* (Singer), 149
misconceptions
 identified through conversations, 159–161
 reteaching misunderstood topics, 162
 targeted teaching, to address, 161–162
mistakes
 benefits of admitting, 13–14
 celebrating mistakes, 22–25
 correcting students' mistakes, 126–127
 "mistakes friendly" classrooms, 22
 modeling of, 17–21
modeling by teachers
 connecting ideas, 111–112
 connecting others' ideas, 113
 getting back on topic, 106–107
 inviting others in, 121–122
 learning from mistakes, 17–21
 navigating disagreements, 130–131

modeling by teachers (*continued*)
   self-awareness, 131–132
   staying on topic, 102–103
Mooney, Carol Garhart, 126
morning meetings and "share time," 18, 34–35, 49–50, 64–65, 104–105
multiple sentences, to support ideas, 58–59

National Council of Teachers of English, 7
noticing and naming
   active listening, 75
   agreeing and disagreeing, 91
   comprehension, 81–82, 83
   connecting ideas, 111–112
   learning from mistakes, 18
   multiple perspectives, 142–143
   new idea introduction, 53–54
   reading people, 120
   paraphrasing, 87
   self-management, 132
   staying on topic, 104–105
   by students for peers, 133
   as tool, 64

openings. *See* initiation of conversation
open spaces in classrooms, 17
optical illusions, 142, 143

paraphrasing, 85–87, 87*f*
participation, encouragement of, 35–37
"pause and breathe," 119–120
pauses, purposeful, 116–117
peers
   inclusion of, 116–124
   learning from, 23–24
   peer assessments, 78
   peer instruction, 160
   peer relationships, 43
"Personal SEL Reflection" (CASEL), 31
perspectives, differing, 140–150. *See also* disagreements
planning future instruction, 159–163

poetry, 149
problem solving, 33–34
processing skills, 89–96, 139-140
prompts
   for conversations, 46
   specific contrasted with open-ended, 157*f*
   targeted, for assessments, 156–159

Quaglia, Russell, 166–167
*Questioning for Classroom Discussion* (Walsh and Sattes), 42
questions
   for clarification, 82–85
   as conversation prompt, 47–51
   encouraging questions, 29–30
   for information, 79–82
   quality of, 48–49
   recording questions, 29–30
   value of "not knowing" and asking questions, 13–14, 25–27, 37–39
quiet students, 116–117

recording of conversations, 68
reflection. *See* processing skills
relationship skills, 33, 134–135
rephrasing, to clarify thoughts, 64–65, 136
responsible decision making, 33–34, 135
Responsive Classroom model, 34
reteaching misunderstood topics, 162
Reverso poetry, 149
rewording, to clarify thoughts, 64–65
risk taking, 13, 26–27, 79–80, 81, 133
Rodgers, Carol, 165
role play, 76, 119–120
routine and structure, 34–35

sample conversations
   about *Drawn Together,* 93–94
   about *Each Kindness,* 62–63
   about economics lesson, 143–144
   about *I Want My Hat Back,* 145–147

sample conversations (*continued*)
    about *Knock, Knock: My Dad's Dream for Me*, 2–4
    about *Our World of Wonders*, 82–83
    about *True or False: Planets*, 5–6
    about weather and the Earth, 66
    to establish context, 80
    and paraphrasing, 86
    and small-group work, 84–85
Sattes, Beth Dankert, 42
science lessons and experiments, 29
Scieszka, Jon, 149
self-assessment
    for students, 59–60, 60*f*, 88–89, 89*f*, 109–110
    for teachers, 99
self-awareness, 31, 101–103, 129–131
self-esteem, 21
self-management skills, 31–32, 101–102, 117, 131–132
Sentence Starters
    clarifying, 67*f*
    comprehending, 88*f*
    connecting ideas, 114*f*
    initiating, 54*f*
    inviting others in, 123*f*
    processing, 94*f*
    seeing other perspectives, 150*f*
    staying on topic, 108, 109*f*
    supporting, 59*f*
*Sharing the Blue Crayon* (Buckley), 18
silences, 116–117
Singer, Marilyn, 149
small groups, 83–84, 118, 161–162
Smith, Dominique, 30, 137
social awareness, 32–33, 132–134
social-emotional skills
    relationship skills, 33, 134–135
    responsible decision making, 33–34, 135
    self-awareness, 31, 101–102, 129–131
    self-esteem, 21
    self-management, 31–32, 101–102, 117, 131–132
    social awareness, 32–33, 132–134

spontaneous conversations, among students, 4
state standards, 7, 90
Steuer, Gabriele, 22
strengths, identified through conversations, 159–161
structure and routine, 34–35
structured practice, 86, 87
student empowerment, 165–167
student-led conversations. *See* conversations
supporting ideas, skills for, 56–61, 136–137
synthesis. *See* processing skills

tangential remarks, 105–106. *See also* focus on topic
task-and-share model, 23–24, 142–143
teachers
    role in conversations, 4
    time spent talking, 16
*They All Saw a Cat* (Wenzel), 148
*The True Story of the Three Little Pigs* (Scieszka), 149
trust, 13, 14–15, 35–37, 41
"turn and talks," 77
*Two Bad Ants* (Van Allsburg), 148

understanding others, skills for, 137–139
unprompted conversations, 104–105

Van Allsburg, Chris, 148
video clips as tool, 75
vulnerability, 26–27

Walsh, Jackie Acree, 42
*We Belong* (Barron and Kinney), 33
Wenzel, Brendan, 148
West, Lucy, 127
*When Aidan Became a Brother* conversation summary, 107–108
writing, as planning tool for students, 51–52

# ABOUT THE AUTHOR

Jennifer Orr is an elementary school teacher in the suburbs of Washington, D.C. She has taught for more than two decades in almost every elementary grade at schools serving highly diverse populations. She has extensive experience working with students who are learning English, students in special education programs, students in advanced academic programs, and students in military families. Throughout her career, she has achieved and renewed National Board Certification; written articles about technology in education, literacy, math, questioning, and more; and presented at state and national conferences on the same topics. Orr is a member of ASCD's Emerging Leader class of 2013. In 2012, Orr won the Kay L. Bitter Award from the International Society for Technology in Education. For nearly a decade, she has been involved with the Northern Virginia Writing Project, serving as a staff member during the Invitational Summer Institute and participating in a wide range of other activities. In addition, Orr has hosted many preservice teachers in her classrooms and mentored multiple new teachers. She has taught elementary literacy courses for graduate students and children's literature for undergraduate students. Orr studied education at Mary Washington College and The University of Virginia, where she earned her master's degree in Social Foundations of Education. Her Twitter account is @jenorr.

## Related ASCD Resources

At the time of publication, the following resources were available (ASCD stock numbers in parentheses):

*All Learning Is Social and Emotional: Helping Students Develop Essential Skills for Classroom and Beyond* by Nancy Frey, Douglas Fisher, and Dominique Smith (#119033)

*The Best Class You Never Taught: How Spider Web Discussion Can Turn Students into Learning Leaders* by Alexis Wiggins (#117017)

*Building a Positive and Supportive Classroom* (Quick Reference Guide) by Julie Causton and Kate MacLeod (#QRG120098)

*Engaging Students in Every Classroom* (Quick Reference Guide) by Susan Hentz and Michelle Vacchio (#QRG120056)

*Giving Students a Say: Smarter Assessment Practices to Empower and Engage* by Myron Dueck (#119013)

*The Formative Five: Fostering Grit, Empathy, and Other Success Skills Every Student Needs* by Thomas Hoerr (#116043)

*Fostering Student Voice* (Quick Reference Guide) by Russell Quaglia and Kristine Fox (#QRG119034)

*Improve Every Lesson Plan with SEL* by Jeffrey Benson (#121057)

*Improving Classroom Discussion* (Quick Reference Guide) by Jackie Acree Walsh (#QRG117053)

*Mindfulness in the Classroom: Strategies for Promoting Concentration, Compassion, and Calm* by Thomas Armstrong (#120018)

*Questioning for Classroom Discussion: Purposeful Speaking, Engaged Listening, Deep Thinking* by Jackie Acree Walsh and Beth Dankert Sattes (#115012)

*Questioning Strategies to Activate Student Thinking* (Quick Reference Guide) by Jackie Acree Walsh (#QRG117054)

*So Each May Soar: The Principles and Practices of Learner-Centered Classrooms* by Carol Ann Tomlinson (#118006)

*We Belong: 50 Strategies to Create Community and Revolutionize Classroom Management* by Laurie Barron and Patti Kinney (#122002)

For up-to-date information about ASCD resources, go to www.ascd.org. You can search the complete archives of *Educational Leadership* magazine at www.ascd.org/el.

For more information, send an email to member@ascd.org; call 1-800-933-2723 or 1-703-578-9600; send a fax to 1-703-575-5400; or write to Information Services, ASCD, 1703 N. Beauregard St., Alexandria, VA 22311-1714 USA.

**DON'T MISS A SINGLE ISSUE OF ASCD'S AWARD-WINNING MAGAZINE.**

If you belong to a Professional Learning Community, you may be looking for a way to get your fellow educators' minds around a complex topic. Why not delve into a relevant theme issue of *Educational Leadership*, the journal written by educators for educators?

Subscribe now, or purchase back issues of ASCD's flagship publication at **www.ascd.org/el**. Discounts on bulk purchases are available.

To see more details about these and other popular issues of *Educational Leadership*, visit **www.ascd.org/el/all**.

2800 Shirlington Road
Suite 1001
Arlington, VA 22206 USA

www.ascd.org/learnmore

www.ingramcontent.com/pod-product-compliance
Lightning Source LLC
Chambersburg PA
CBHW070553010526
44118CB00012B/1310